Praise for *How Old Am I In Dog Years?*

"The life examined is worth living – especially if it's this deep and funny."

Willie Nelson, singer, songwriter, author

"If you want to stay funny and fabulous during the third act of life, take Susan Goldfein along. She's the hilarious BFF who's thinking what you're thinking – about everything from gray hair to granny names – and she's not afraid to write it."

Jan Tuckwood, presentation editor, *The Palm Beach Post*

"Just when we think no one 'gets it' anymore, there comes along a new voice that excavates and skewers. A fresh sensibility illuminating a well-beaten path. Susan Goldfein's voice, welcoming yet tart, casts the Golden Years as 'antic realism,' as well as being a manual for everyone on their way to seniority. This book will cause a reader to say, 'I'll have what she's writing.'"

Julie Gilbert, novelist, biographer, playwright, and teacher

"Susan observes 'life from the other side of the hill' with wit, style, insight, and great good humor. You'll be smiling, laughing, and nodding in recognition."

William Hayes, producing artistic director,

Dear Jane & Dick

Thank you so much
for your support.

Best,
Susan

HOW OLD AM I

IN DOG YEARS?

HOW OLD AM I IN DOG YEARS?

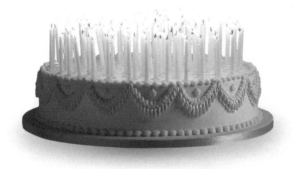

*and other thoughts about life
from the far side of the hill*

SUSAN GOLDFEIN

TWO HARBORS PRESS, MINNEAPOLIS

Two Harbors Press
322 First Avenue N, 5th floor
Minneapolis, MN 55401
612.455.2293
www.TwoHarborsPress.com

The essays in this collection have previously appeared on the author's blog 1000thingstosaybeforeidie.com

The prologue has previously appeared in the *Palm Beach Post*.

ISBN-13: 978-1-63413-392-0
LCCN: 2015935688

Distributed by Itasca Books

Cover Design by Lois Stanfield
Typeset by Mary K. Ross
Edited by Robert Christian Schmidt

Printed in the United States of America

FOR JULIE AND LARRY

CONTENTS

Prologue // xiii

Contents

PROLOGUE

What Shall I Do All Day?
(or, How I Learned to Stop Worrying
and Start Blogging)

So it was Monday morning, and there I was. Instead of rushing off to work, I was lingering over my second cup of coffee and contemplating the blessings of my recent retirement.

Listed among those blessings was the fact that I no longer had to settle for instant oatmeal. My membership in AARP was legitimized. I had the option to linger. And I finally had time to do all those things I'd always wanted to do. What were they again?

Despite all the wonderful perks that bolstered my retiree status, I recognized with trepidation that life as I knew it was radically changed. Giving up my career was a little like experiencing the empty-nest syndrome all over again, but without the kid coming home with a load of dirty laundry. I was deeply saddened by the thought that I might never again be required to multitask.

No longer was I "Dr. Susan," speech pathologist, consultant, and adjunct professor. (Just as an aside, I would have preferred using my middle name, Ruth, but a short woman with an accent had already taken it.) The challenge of a full-time job had been replaced by the challenge of discovering my comfort zone in this new phase of my life.

I remembered once reading an announcement about a seminar on "Successful Retirement." I couldn't help but wonder if the term "successful retirement" implied that failure was a possibility? For me, failure was not an option. For a moment, I thought that, perhaps, I should consider signing up for one of those workshops without delay.

Instead, for guidance, I turned to reading affirming articles about retirement. I tried to be reassured by the promise that there were still "endless possibilities for fulfillment." I was informed that I was not merely "retiring." I was experiencing a passage. I was transitioning. I had choices. I could break free, or launch, or reinvent myself. But, first, I had to figure out which was the right path for me. Quite frankly, it all sounded positively exhausting.

I decided to table the existential questions for the moment in order to deal with a more immediate concern. How should I fill the void? What would I do on that Monday, the first day of the rest of my life?

Falling back on the organizational skills that had catapulted me to the top of my game professionally, as well as efficiently guiding me through the supermarket, I took out pad and pen, and began making a list:

◊   clear breakfast dishes;

◊   inquire after grandchildren;

◊   take shower;

◊   get dressed.

That might use up about forty minutes; only 550 more to go.

Getting dressed. There was a conundrum. What does a retired person wear? Does it matter? Whom would I see on my first day of retirement, and who would see me? My closet was top-heavy with business attire, which no longer seemed appropriate now that every day was casual Friday.

I occupied the afternoon by going to the dry cleaners, getting the car washed, doing laundry, and shopping for dinner. Things that I had previously managed to squeeze into a small segment of a working woman's schedule were now stretched to fill an entire day.

I told myself that this would never do. I could not spend my time in this manner. I was at risk for becoming marginalized. If this continued, people would no longer find me interesting. Did I care? I hoped I didn't, but I probably did.

And all the books said I was supposed to be discovering my creativity and passion, releasing my alter ego. The pressure was immense. I wasn't sure I could handle this retirement thing. I seriously considered returning to work.

But, gradually, I got a grip. I gave up self-help articles and began perusing catalogs, looking for activities more interesting than vacuuming dog hair. I rejected a gardening class. I wanted to smell the roses, not plant them. And my last attempt at yoga had resulted in a series of chiropractic adjustments.

Salvation came in the form of a writing class for beginners. I had once been a good writer, before graduate school and a profession got in the way, and I wondered if I still had the stuff.

It turned out to be one of the best decisions I've ever made. I suddenly had a new peer group, a community of fledgling writers like myself, creating short stories, novels, or memoirs.

My own voice seemed to resonate best with humorous personal essays. I began writing about my marriage, about becoming an "older" woman, about friendships, consumerism, the movies, and about how, one summer, the birds ate my car. This was a very fruitful endeavor. I was able to further develop two of my essential talents: writing and complaining.

Eventually, I decided to create my own website and began posting my essays on line.

With that initiative in place, I felt a keen sense of accomplishment. I had achieved successful retirement status. I had transitioned, broken free. I was launched and reinvented. I was a blogger! I would take my place beside other authors who had turned kvetching into a literary genre.

Prologue

I am now three years into my little project, and I have no plans to quit any time soon. I now view retirement as a gift. It has given me the time to see the world around me with a fresh eye and find fodder for my essays in places I would never have thought to look. The pratfalls that life presents us on a daily basis have hardly been exhausted, and I intend to comment on all of them.

HAPPILY EVER AFTER

E-Male

Thank you, Bill Gates. Thank you, Steve Jobs. You may have saved my marriage. Because of you, my husband and I hardly argue any more. That is because we hardly talk anymore. Instead, we send each other abbreviated, misspelled, unpunctuated messages via email and texting.

"Honey," I write in an email from my computer to his PDA, "I made a date for us to go out with Bob and Jane this Saturday night. Put it in your iPhone." I communicate this to him electronically, because I know what I have done will not make him happy.

He does not care for the company of Bob and Jane, but I could put them off no longer. If I tell him this in person, I have to watch him roll his eyes, drop his head, grimace, and altogether act like I have just invited Hitler for brunch. This will aggravate me, because he is not being a good sport about my old high school best friend with whom I have recently reunited. Then I will remind him about the drunken reunion I sat through with his obnoxious fraternity brothers and their boring wives, and *viol*à! We're having an argument.

Instead, I receive a written response which says: "If I haf 2!" I am reasonably certain he has gone through his annoying gestural routine before sending me his answer, but only the dog knows for sure. And I'm not asking.

Then there was the time I backed the new car into a tree. "Hun," I text, "I'll b late. Car accident." And I quickly turned off my cell phone. Had I called him to tell him this, or waited until I got home, my "hun" would have reacted similarly to his tribesman Attila. This, of course, would have reduced me to a pathetic, weepy little woman, which in turn would have resulted in an outpouring of counterattacks as soon as I had regained my composure.

Fortunately, none of that has to happen anymore. Instead, my "accident" text message raised just enough concern that by the time I got home he was so happy to see me safe and sound that the dangling rear bumper was of little consequence.

I am pleased to say that my new e-marriage is flourishing. We are currently 4G, but are seriously considering a whole new level of happiness as a 5G couple. I feel giddy as I anticipate the possibilities!

I would be less than honest, however, if I don't report that there is a downside to all this electronic passion. Since my husband switched his PDA from a Blackberry to an iPhone, I have not seen his face. The machine constantly calls to him with whooshes, beeps, pings, and rings, and he cannot help but respond. When that is not happening, he is emailing, texting, phoning, reading headlines, or trying to figure out what else the damn thing can do. It's been three weeks now. I am starting to forget what he looks like, but I am very well acquainted with the bald spot on top of his head.

I realize that progress is not without sacrifice. Even so, occasional eye contact would still be nice.

Who knows? Maybe there's an app for that!

Losing Streak

It's as inevitable as the changing of the seasons, as predictable as the ebb and flow of the tides, as constant as the sunrise in the morning. It is its own force of nature, but with a human voice—the daily cry from the upstairs bedroom: "Honey, I can't find my glasses!"

Did I see them? Did I move them? Did I take them? I must have, otherwise they would be exactly where he left them, wherever that was. So I go upstairs, trying to ignore the implication that somehow this is all my fault, and help him retrace his steps. When did he last have them? What did he do after that? Where has he already searched? The answer to the last question is less than helpful, of course, because he could never find his glasses without his glasses. "Oh, look," I say as I lift the newspaper he has just set down, revealing the glasses, "they just crawled right under here."

Okay, so I exaggerate. It's not *always* the glasses. Another morning it was "The Case of the Missing Letter." The letter in question had vanished from the *exact* spot (so sure was he) where it had been placed. "The housekeeper must have moved it," he said in a manner that suggested she had no business rearranging any of his valuable documents, even if they were carelessly strewn around the room. I assured him that it couldn't have been her because the housekeeper is, in fact, terrified of the stacks of paper that clutter the top of his desk, and doesn't enter his office at all. Instead, she stands at the doorway with a long-handled duster and leans in as far as she can. Once again engaging my highly evolved feminine search techniques, I find the letter, which had miraculously walked across the room, climbed up the table leg, and laid itself down near the telephone. (How else could it have possibly gotten there?)

It must be wonderful to be filled with such certainty that you are incapable of erring, of slipping up, of actually losing something all on your own. I wouldn't know. I am only a woman, and not possessed of male DNA. But I am becoming more convinced that this is an age-old issue that, in fact, might have vexed Eve as she helped Adam search for his fig leaf, the loss of which was something else to blame on the snake. (Poor thing, but then, who else was there?)

I admit that I waste a lot of time thinking about this, time I could be spending looking for his vanished credit card, which I probably removed from his billfold and used to go shopping, even though I have a card of my own, or the golf club that was definitely in the trunk of the car. But I believe I have finally figured out the logic behind the attitude. It goes like this:

1. Flawless men don't lose or misplace things.

2. I am a flawless man.

3. Therefore, if I can't find something, it's someone else's fault.

This syllogism, though specious at best, then becomes the basis for the following:

◊ "There's only one glove. Who took the other one?"

◊ "I couldn't have lost that expensive umbrella. I don't do things like that."

◊ "I distinctly remember packing my raincoat. Why isn't it here?"

As irritating as this outlook can be, I actually feel sorry for men. Being flawless can put such pressure on a person. Perhaps all perfect males should follow the example set by some of our congressional leaders, and sign a pledge. They would vow to lower their expectations and accept their human foibles. I'm sure my husband would be willing to add his name—just as soon as he figures out who took his pen.

Code Red: Man in the Kitchen!

Question: What's the scariest thing that a wife of forty years might hear from her husband?

(No, it's not "I'm leaving you for a younger woman," though that might be preferable to the true correct response.)

Answer: "Honey, at the end of the year, I'm going to retire."

Question: What's the scariest thing that a wife of forty years might catch her retired husband doing?

(No, it's not logging on to Internet porn, though, again, that might be preferable.)

Answer: Sitting on the couch in front of the TV screen in the middle of the day watching *Iron Chef*!

"Honey," he says, ignoring the terror in your eyes as he looks up and sees you standing there, "I'm going to try my hand at cooking."

"How about something less messy, like stamp collecting?" you timidly suggest while visions of food stains on your marble counter tops dance menacingly in your head.

"It doesn't look so hard," he says. "What if I prepare dinner for us tomorrow? You go out and enjoy yourself, and let me surprise you with a wonderful meal when you get home."

"Okay," you agree in your best less-than-enthusiastic-but-trying-to-be-supportive voice.

Later that night, do you really hear fire engine sirens approaching your house, or is it a nightmare about your kitchen burning?

He's out of bed before you in the morning and you find him in the kitchen surrounded by all thirty of your cookbooks, enthusiastically wetting his thumb and flipping the pages.

"Aha," he says, "I think I've found just the thing. I'm going grocery shopping. You have a great day!"

You decide to calm yourself with a visit to a day spa. But, first, you return the other twenty-nine cookbooks to the shelf. Who expects the Iron Chef to clean up after himself?

Your cell phone rings just as you are about to have your facial.

"Hi, honey, sorry to bother you, but I need a mixing bowl. Where do you keep them?"

"They're in the cabinet below the toaster oven."

"Oh, yes, I see them. But why do you keep them there? Wouldn't it be better to keep them in the cabinet next to the refrigerator? That way you can…"

His voice trails off as you remove the phone from your ear. You are at a spa. You do not want to get angry as you listen to Mr. Micromanager's suggestions for reorganizing *your* kitchen!

You lie quietly and breathe deeply. The cosmetologist has applied a soothing mud pack to your face, and has left the room. Soft music is playing. Your phone rings again. You know you shouldn't answer it, but you do. His voice again.

"What's a whisk?"

"A whisk is what you use to whip things, like eggs."

"Do we have one?"

"Yes, we do. It's in the utensil holder near the stove."

"What's it look like?"

"What's it look like?" How do you explain what a whisk looks like? Couldn't he ask me to describe something less complicated, like a spatula? You can feel the mud cracking on your face as you grimace. You know you will never forgive him if the crevices imprint additional wrinkles on your skin.

"Well, the top is kind of oval-shaped and it has these wires—"

"Thanks, honey, I think I have it. Bye now."

You're fantasizing in the vibrating pedicure chair when your cell phone beckons once again. Your inner voice is telling you not to answer, but you do. Of course, it's him.

"Honey, there's something wrong with the food processor."

"Did you find the right blade?" you ask.

"Of course I did," he says indignantly. "But when I pushed the button, the stuff just went all over the counter."

"Did you have the cover on?"

"Oh," he says, dropping the indignation, "guess I forgot the cover."

"Don't worry," you say, noting the discouragement in his voice. "Anyone could have made that mistake."

The chair continues to vibrate, but your fantasies have definitely switched gears.

The last phone call comes when you are driving, having finally found the courage to return home.

"Hi, it's me."

What a surprise!

"Can you do me a big favor? This dish I'm surprising you with, *Chicken ala Valenciana Poblana*, I forgot one little ingredient. Could you stop on your way home and get it for me?"

"Sure," you say, "what is it?"

"The chicken."

You arrive home, enter the kitchen, and hand him the poultry. You look around and see that things are not as bad as you had imagined. They are much, *much* worse.

At 10:30 pm, after closing the door on the devastation that used to be your kitchen, you are finally sitting down to dinner. Actually not bad for a first effort. You compliment your husband, but hope that you don't sound *too* encouraging.

With the last bite in his mouth, he states that this cooking thing is exhausting and he is going to bed, not even giving you the opportunity to suggest that, as an alternative, he might enroll for bridge lessons.

By one in the morning, you have finished loading the dishwasher and have scrubbed every pot and pan that you own. The last bit of dried sauce residue has been scraped off the floor. Where are dogs when you need them? Probably sleeping peacefully with *him*. You decide that you'll wait until morning to tackle the ceiling. Apparently dish-washing was not a part of the deal. But, again, who expects the Iron Chef to clean up after himself?

Remote Possibilities

What I'm about to say is not exactly breaking news. It is something that every wife and female significant other knows only too well. While we can congratulate ourselves on having made great strides in the fight for equality with males in many arenas, there remains at least one battle zone where men are holding fast. And I do mean holding fast. It might as well be a logo on a victory banner. A tightly clenched masculine fist, with fingers possessively wrapped around the TV remote control.

The origins of a man's inalienable right to dominate TV viewing is unclear to me. But no matter. I give up. I give in. I have moved on to assert myself in other areas, like the setting on the air conditioning, or which side of the bed is unarguably mine. But there are evenings in the TV room when I seriously consider rebellion.

I present two scenarios:

My husband and I have finished eating dinner, and it's time for relocation. I relocate into the kitchen to do the cleaning up, and he relocates onto his favorite chair in front of our amply sized flat-screen TV with the state-of-the art sound system. I can clearly hear the state-of-the-art sound system above the loud sounds of the water running in the sink, the clanging of the pot that I am trying to clean, and the dogs noisily rearranging the dishes in the dishwasher as they try to lick off the last piece of food residue. I am finally finished and look forward to relaxing for an hour or two while watching my favorite TV shows. I mean to ask my husband if he wouldn't mind lowering the volume a bit, but I find him fast asleep in his favorite chair with the TV remote, as represented on the victory banner, clenched tightly in his fist.

I'm a sensitive person. I don't want to disturb him. But it's come down to a choice between his nap and my ear drums. Potential hearing loss trumps snoozing any time. I try to be gentle, but did you ever try to pry a delicious, meaty bone out of a dog's mouth? Even if you haven't, I'm sure you get what I mean. Of course I wake him up, and of course he is upset with me. I ask a simple question. "Why can't you leave the remote on the table in neutral territory?" He looks at me like I have just suggested he donate a kidney.

Or I enter the room and a serious drama is being played out on the TV screen. The actors are all beautiful and very emotive. It is a tragedy of some sort and people are crying. Sad music is playing the background. I could easily become absorbed, except for one little drawback: everyone is speaking Spanish. My husband has been lying on the couch, channelsurfing. He apparently wiped-out at Telemundo. And where is the remote control? Resting peacefully on top of the family jewels. I wonder what the cost would be of trying to excise it from that portion of his anatomy, and decide it would be more prudent to go bungee-jumping.

Perhaps it is too late for my generation of women to change the sexual politics of controlling the remote. Had we foreseen our bondage, we would have insisted on a "prenup" guaranteeing equal-opportunity clicker management. But I see a brighter day ahead for my younger sisters. I read in the *New York Times* recently that the device as we know it may soon be obsolete, and could be replaced by another that interfaces with the TV via brain power.

I grin as I imagine how that will level the playing field, and dare I suggest, even shift the advantage?

Driver's Ed

There has been an amendment to my marriage contract. I'm not referring to a legal document that was signed in the presence of a lawyer or a rabbi who may or may not have also been a notary, but an informal set of conventions that have evolved over time in the partnership.

Every marriage has one. It usually includes a tacit or explicit division of responsibilities that permits the union to function more or less efficiently on a daily basis. For example, in my marriage, I'm in charge of such details as making sure we don't run out of toilet paper, seeing to it that the dogs are fed twice daily, changing light bulbs, and brewing coffee in the morning. My husband, as we have discussed, is in charge of the remote control.

And, for most of our time together, he has been the family driver. Until recently.

I am thankful to say that the change did not come about due to an illness or a serious incapacity. But, rather, it began as a practical matter having to do with whose eyesight was better after dark: mine.

While I'm sure there was some reluctance on my husband's part to relinquish control of the steering wheel to the little woman, it had to be done. And there were definitely benefits which came with the change which helped to assuage his male ego, benefits like, perhaps, a little more wine with dinner, and a catnap on the way home from the movies.

The perks of being a passenger obviously did not go unnoticed by my husband, for soon there were seemingly innocent requests to be chauffeured in full sunlight. Usually something like, "Could you drive? I have to make a few calls," as he reached into his pocket for the iPhone.

Let me state that I have no objection to change. Change can be healthy. It can signify that, like the Constitution, or your Facebook page, the marriage contract is a living document, capable of adapting to the needs of the present day. And I don't mind driving.

It's the driving lessons I can do without!

I have my first lesson as we are about to set out to visit some friends on a Saturday afternoon.

"You drive," he says. "I have to return some emails." Out comes the iPhone as I slip into the driver's seat.

"Why are you backing out of the garage like that?" he asks.

"Like what?" I reply.

"You're turning the steering wheel twice, when I only have to turn it once."

"So, did I hit anything?"

He returns to his emails as I successfully pull out of our driveway.

I apply the brakes as we come to a red light.

"You waited too long. You're going to ruin the brake linings."

"I have been driving since 1959 and all my brakes' linings have always been pristine," I remind him.

"Well, it's dangerous to wait so long. You can hit the guy in front of you."

I also remind him that the only person in the car to have recently caused a fender-bender was him. Suddenly, it's time for him to make another phone call.

"Why are you staying in this lane?" he asks as he finally notices that we have entered the highway. "All the other lanes are moving faster."

"Do you not see the fourteen-wheeler barreling down on my left?" I reply. "If I pull out now we're going to ruin a lot more than the brake linings."

"Well, get out of this lane as soon as you can. You know I can't stand driving in slow traffic."

"Yes," I hiss between clenched teeth, "but you're *not* driving. Isn't there someone you need to text?"

We arrive in our friends' neighborhood without further comment, and I assume the driving lesson has ended. I head toward a parking space.

"Park there," he says, his finger wagging at a different spot.

"Why?" I ask.

"It's better."

In spite of the fact that I was contemplating a divorce, we had a cheery afternoon, followed by dinner at a lovely restaurant.

"How's the wine?" I ask him as I'm sipping my club soda.

"Quite good," he answers.

"So have a little more," I innocently encourage.

Five minutes into the return trip, my darling falls asleep. Anticipating a peaceful ride home, I pray that he does not begin to snore. I'm lucky this time. I ride in blessed silence.

I breathe a sigh of relief as I pull the car into our garage when, suddenly, Lazarus beside me strongly recommends that I back out and try it again.

Only, this time, I should turn the wheel more to the right so that when he backs out in the morning, he won't knock off the side-view mirror like he did last time—which was all my fault because I didn't park correctly.

And so the journey ends as it began.

Looking ahead, I can see that this new arrangement in our marriage is going to be a challenge. There is nothing worse than a backseat driver who is sitting right next to you. I wonder if there's a law against forcing your passenger to ride in the trunk. Whatever the penalty is, it may be worth it. It has to be a lesser offense than murder.

Mea Culpa

This is so awkward!

The situation in which I currently find myself is both embarrassing and humbling. But I must be strong and endure the humiliation of a public confession.

In prior essays, I have written about the tiny, but not insignificant, imperfections in my married life. I have shared the fact that my husband constantly loses things, makes a mess in the kitchen, hogs the remote control, and, more recently, how he micro-manages my driving. Hang on to that last one. It has relevance to what follows.

The story begins when we were driving to meet some friends for dinner. Or, I should say, I was driving, he was managing.

"Get off at the next exit," was his latest instruction, as if I hadn't already been to their home at least ten times. And my long-term memory is still intact, thank you very much!

Exiting the highway went smoothly. So did the drive toward the intersection where he told me I had to make a left turn, again demonstrating lack of confidence in either my long-term memory, or my sense of direction. (The latter, just between you and me, would be warranted.)

It was then that the unthinkable happened. As I steered over to the left lane, I failed to notice the concrete median that had absolutely no business being where it was—and drove the car right over it!

Terrible grinding and crunching noises ensued. The car groaned and creaked and lurched forward with short, reluctant jerks until I managed to get it off the road and into a parking area. By then, the dashboard was ablaze with lights of every color. Icons appeared showing little oil cans, bright tiny engines, water droplets, and pictures of other auto parts sitting under the hood that are unidentifiable by the lay person. Clearly, anything that could possibly go wrong, had.

There is no subtle way to put this, so I will come right out with it: *I wrecked his car!*

I will not bore you with the details of what followed, except to say that our gracious friends came to our rescue, helped us in securing a tow truck, and later, after a delayed dinner, drove us home.

I know what you're thinking. Don't be afraid to ask. How did my husband react to my poor grasp of spatial relations and the loss of his car? Did he shout stupid phrases at me, like "How could you do this?" or "How could you not see that curb?" or "Maybe you need glasses?"

No, it was much worse. He was gentle. He was sympathetic. He was supportive. He never raised his voice. He comforted me, telling me "These things happen. It was an accident. Luckily, no one was hurt." He assured me that the road was confusing and unfamiliar, that *Consumer Reports* had given the car the top rating for models built too low to the ground. How sweet was he! How amazingly understanding. How *utterly* guilt-provoking!

He handled the aftermath calmly and confidently, calling the insurance company, the repair shop, the auto rental dealer. I waited and waited for the shoe to drop, but it never did.

In a sense of fairness, I thought it only right to share his kindness with you, as I do his foibles. It is part of my self-imposed penance, and much less of a fashion faux pas than wearing sackcloth in Palm Beach.

We found out that the car was totaled. Not good news. But was that a glint of excitement in his eye as he informed me that he would now have to shop for a brand new one?

As for me, this little episode resulted in two sleepless nights, where I lay awake wondering how I could have been so stupid. And do you know the biggest frustration about this entire episode? Because my husband was so very, very nice, there was no way to manipulate the circumstances and figure out how any of this could have possibly been his fault.

Bagel Sunday

Minutes before we humans begin to stir in our beds, the dogs know. They are pacing around the room, instead of lying quietly on the floor as is their way on every other morning, patiently waiting for signs that the day has officially begun. This morning they are awake and alert, with two sets of imploring eyes fixed on us, as if their intensity alone could levitate us from the bed. Then, when it is my husband, and not I, who is the first to respond, to sit up and plant two feet on the floor, they are certain. It is Sunday and my old, arthritic Yellow Labrador retrievers begin leaping with joy!

Mah nishtanah, I want to say to my dogs. *What makes this day different from all other days?* How do you know it's Sunday? I scrutinize my bedroom for physical evidence. The clock reads about seven o'clock, the same time we awaken every morning. The same amount of light slips in between the crack in the draperies covering our east-facing windows. There are no unusual sounds; no church bells can be heard. And yet they know.

They follow him to the bathroom and back to the bedroom, so closely that he is barely able to pull up his pants or get his shoes on. They are impatient as he brushes his teeth. Droplets of saliva on the floor are signs of their anticipation. Finally he is ready, and the dialogue begins.

"Davis, Bette, do you know what day this is? Do you?"

(Yes, their names are Bette and Davis.)

Whine. Bark. Leap. Pant. Salivate.

"It's Sunday. Sunday is bagel day. Come on, let's go get a bagel!"

Amid unbridled excitement and a flurry of dog fur, the three march out of the bedroom, down the stairs, and into the car to carry out their mission: bring home the Sunday bagels, and—of course—eat one or two along the way.

Over the past ten years, knowledge of our little Sunday ritual has spread to our friends and family. We are teased about the sanctity we have bestowed on this occasion. His friends know better than to ask my husband for an early golf date on a Sunday morning. Sunday brunch is out of the question. We are gently mocked, but at the same time I sense a degree of envy. We have succeeded in creating a bit of fun. A piece of silliness that is guaranteed to lighten our hearts and ensure that we laugh at least once a week. It is, after all, in the best weekend tradition—whether your Sabbath is celebrated on Saturday or Sunday— that there is one day when thoughts are diverted from mundane concerns.

Our grandchildren, when we are with them over a weekend, become part of the Sunday practice. Up early, they catch Papa just as he and the dogs are about to leave, and place their orders. Little Jack wants a rainbow bagel; Alexandra wants plain; Leah and Kira like sesame; and Chloe, well, she's not sure she wants one at all. We delight in their participation and their innocent, sweet acceptance of Bagel Day as a completely normal phenomenon.

I like to think we are giving them a precious memory. One day, when they are grown and we are no longer here, they will no doubt eat a bagel. They will think of their grandfather driving off in the car each week with Bette and Davis in the back, their mouths open and tongues protruding, knowing unquestionably that it's Bagel Sunday.

The Road Not Taken

It was my personal opinion that if your car had a GPS, your marriage had at least a fifty percent better chance of lasting than the national average. I confess that this conclusion was not based on a government-sponsored scientific research study, but rather on anecdotal evidence gathered from years of road trips with two different husbands. I offer the fact that I even had two different husbands as support for my hypothesis.

Second only to an argument about the air conditioner setting, there is nothing more conducive to a shout fest than riding in a car with your spouse on your way to a location neither of you had ever been.

Prior to the GPS, one of you would be driving, the other holding the map. In my case, the map was usually upside down. Map reading is not a skill that is on my resume. The driver (him) relying on the map reader (me) as the car approached the fork in the road, could get very hot under the collar while I was still struggling to determine if the road in question was the pink one or the green one.

"Don't you see it?" his words would say, while the message conveyed by the tone of his voice was "Are you blind or stupid?" While not so good at map reading, I was very good at interpreting tones of voices. "Don't yell at me," I would retaliate. "It's not my fault if the mapmaker forgot to include this intersection."

"I'm not yelling at you!"

"Yes you are!"

"No I'm not. Let me see that."

"It's not here, I tell you."

"It has to be. Give me the map; I'll find it!" Implicit in that last remark is "You're a dodo!"

I fight back the tears.

While reminiscing about the past does give rise to a certain nostalgia surrounding the old-fashioned map fight, I definitely do not want to resurrect the good old days. Instead, I embrace the introduction of the GPS in automobiles.

Unlike map reading, I have actually conquered GPS technology and, as a result, I am no longer afraid of it. I cannot say the same about maps. Rather, I bless it for taking the guesswork out of travel. And for freeing us to argue about more important things, like the air conditioner setting. Because of my GPS, I find car trips infinitely more relaxing than they used to be.

At least they were until my husband, the second and—as yet—current one, began having arguments with the disembodied female voice.

It all started one evening when we were meeting some friends for dinner at a place where we had never been. No problem. The GPS has given me heretofore unknown confidence to take on new destinations.

I proudly program the system with the address, and we are on our way. As usual, I'm driving and my husband is engrossed in his iPhone.

All is going well until he puts the phone away and decides to start paying attention to the route on which we're traveling. He confirms that the GPS is doing a good job because this is the way he would have gone. *What a huge relief!*

We're approaching an intersection. "In half a mile, prepare to turn right," the voice informs me. I'm about to engage my directional signal.

"That's wrong," my husband suddenly proclaims. "We should go straight."

I become aware of a tightness in the back of my neck and realize it's the return of the old tension from the map reading days. I am forced to render a decision. *Husband or GPS?* Although I'm not inclined to consider a third spouse, I take a risk and choose the GPS. "Sorry, honey," I say, "but let's try it her way," as I signal for a right turn. He begrudgingly agrees, still claiming that it makes no sense. I imagine the GPS winking at me.

I'm unprepared for the second episode of disagreement, yet it occurs. "This time, I know I'm right," he swears. "Go straight." Not wanting to push my luck, I obey.

This action, of course, agitates the GPS, which begins sputtering "route recalculation, route recalculation." As I further ignore her demand that I make an immediate U-turn, she says it again. This time I imagine that her voice has become surly. She is clearly pissed. And I am losing my mind.

Later that night, when I can't sleep, I relive the events of the evening. The fact that we reached our destination and my husband had actually been correct in the second dispute will only encourage further challenges. The future I had envisioned with no more road trip tension is now threatened. I cherish my husband, but I refuse to relinquish my GPS.

If the two of them really love me, they won't make me choose!

How to Disturb the Peace

Looking over the kitchen counter, I can see my husband. He is in the living room, sitting in his favorite chair, reading the newspaper, and leisurely enjoying his second cup of coffee. It is early morning, and he's still in his pj's, bath robe, and slippers. It is one of those days when he doesn't have to rush off to work. The dogs are curled up at his feet, partially out of love. The other part is the hope that some crumbs from breakfast will fall from his lap.

Although this scenario is one that has become entirely familiar to me, on this particular morning I am suddenly overwhelmed by a warm glow which I'm fairly certain is not a lingering hot flash.

I am moved to take my own second cup of coffee, walk into the living room, and sit in the adjacent chair. I am eager to share the beautiful thoughts that have taken roost in my otherwise foggy morning brain. Eventually he notices that the space next to his is occupied.

"What's up?" he queries.

"Nothing much," I reply. "I was just appreciating how very lucky we are to be in this moment."

"What do you mean?"

"You, me, together in this wonderful environment, being able to share this sense of peace and wellbeing. We should not take such things for granted."

"You're right."

For a moment I am speechless. He is actually agreeing with me. Bolstered by his words, I continue.

"Perhaps we should take a few minutes each morning and give expression to our good fortune."

"You mean, actually discuss that I can still read the paper?"

"No, it's bigger than that. It's like we've been given a gift or something."

"Just kidding. I know what you mean, and I agree. Let's do it."

So, on that first morning of the rest of our lives, we took the time to put our warmest feelings into words.

On the third morning of the rest of our lives, we are still at it. I am beginning to discern a possible trend.

"This is so nice," I say. "We should call it something."

"You mean, like give it a name?"

"Yes, like our 'Reflection Time,' or something like that."

"'Reflection time'? I don't like that. Too new-agey."

"OK, then you come up with something."

"How about 'Gratitude Time'?"

"Don't like that. Too 'Twelve Step.' How about 'Affirmation Time'?" I suggest, beginning to feel less and less grateful for the discussion.

"Definitely not! Straight out of pop psychology!"

Is it my imagination or am I starting to sense some tension in the air as we continue with this naming debate?

"'I'm OK, you're OK'?" I offer.

"Too transactional. We need something that captures the mood. I have the perfect word, serenity. Let's call it our 'Serenity Time.'"

"I could never call it that!" say I with alarm.

"Why not?"

"Because all the time we're supposed to be loving, I'll be thinking of incontinence."

I think he just rolled his eyes at me.

"These moments are a blessing, like the Sabbath. Let's call it our daily dose of Shabbos."

"Way too Jewish," he counters.

"OK, then, a time of Thanksgiving?"

"Much too Christian."

Fortunately, we skipped right over Muslim, Hindu, and Mormon.

"How come you never like any of my ideas?" I whine.

"None of them feel right to me."

"You think yours are better?"

"Well, yes, I do," he asserts.

"Why do you always have to be right?"

"I'm not always right. Except when I am."

"Just once, can't you agree with anything I say?" whining again.

"That's an overstatement. Didn't I agree with you last night?"

"Oh, yeah? About what?"

"That you overcooked the hamburgers."

I didn't see that coming. I almost laugh, until I realize we're in an argument.

"Very funny. Next time *you* cook the hamburgers."

"OK, I will."

"Fine!"

"Fine!"

And with those profound exclamations, he returns to his newspaper and I to the kitchen, where I proceed to make a lot of unnecessary noise by clanging the breakfast dishes. Only our dogs are quiet and unperturbed. I realize that they are, in some ways, more fortunate than we. Unlike humans, they do not have the power of speech, and thus are much less likely to ruin a moment of Zen.

Lord, Won't You Buy Me a Mercedes-Benz...

It's October, and, adhering to the biannual rhythm of our recent life, we have returned to Florida. The flight, fortunately, was uneventful, and we arrived, as scheduled, on the same Saturday on which we boarded the plane. The dogs arrived on Sunday, driven from Connecticut by their faithful friend and chauffeur, Kevin, who has been driving them for many years. (We have made the drive ourselves on three occasions, but between map reading and driver's ed courses, we have decided our marriage has a better chance of survival if we avoid lengthy car trips.)

After unpacking the smashed cartons of wrinkled clothing already delivered by UPS, and calling an endless list of service people to find out why: 1) some of our plants had died; 2) all of our outdoor lights weren't working; 3) our barbecue grill decided to shut down; and, 4) we had no TV reception, we finally settled in.

But the true highlight of our arrival was that, on Monday, my husband was to pick up his brand new car. (To learn why he needed a brand new car, I refer you to "Mea Culpa," above.)

His choice of a new vehicle was by no means haphazard, having devoted much of his summer in pursuit of the ideal machine. He wanted a convertible.

He felt that life in Florida required a convertible. I, on the other hand, don't like riding around in a tanning booth, and would much rather have a roof over my head until the sun goes down.

I watched as all of his lawyerly intensity was brought to bear on this project. I was in awe of how many articles he read, how many phone calls he made, how many test drives he took, and how many eager car salesmen pursued him. He gained so much knowledge that, ultimately, he could quote the amount of backseat legroom and the cubic feet of trunk space for every major brand. He couldn't have been more thorough if he had been given a research grant from *Consumer Reports*!

In the end, he chose the car of his dreams—a Mercedes-Benz convertible. It is a beautiful, sexy car, pearl white with a dark brown top and plush black and brown leather seats. This is no male midlife crisis flashy sports bimbo. She is a sophisticated lady appropriate for "a man of a certain age."

So, on Monday, I drove my eager husband to the car dealership. We shook hands with the salesman, the manager, the finance guy, the detailer, and the receptionist who offered us a bottle of Mercedes-Benz water.

I gushed over our new hi-tech means of transportation, and stayed long enough for an explanation of the unique and innovative ways to unlock the door and start the engine. I never knew that keys were so yesterday!

I recognized that this car would require not just a single tutorial, but an entire course in German ingenuity. With that, I said my good-byes and left him, wishing him the best of luck on the journey home.

Four hours later, he walked through the door looking utterly exhausted. It was obvious that he was suffering from information overload.

The next day, I joined him for our maiden voyage together. He was excited to show me all of the car's magical features. Agent 007 touched a button, and I watched as the rear end opened and closed to swallow the convertible top, then opened again to spit it back out. Windows went down, wind screens popped up. I gasped as the self-adjusting seat belt gave me the Heimlich maneuver.

He showed me all the portals where you can plug in your iPhone, your iPod, your lap top. A regular surge protector on wheels.

When he put the car in reverse, the dash board camera gave us a 360-degree view of the world, making windows completely obsolete. Warning sensors beep, I was informed, if you are too close to anything in any direction at all. Nothing and no one is getting near this baby without permission! My husband wanted to show me more, but this was all that he could remember.

One thing about buying a luxury car: it comes with a concierge. A person from the dealership actually came to our home on two occasions for a refresher course. He also programmed the car to open and close our garage door. *Big deal! I'd be more impressed if it could carry in the groceries.*

Perhaps the gadget that gives my husband the most joy is the voice recognition feature, although this will take a while to conquer completely. On a recent ride together, he instructed the magic genie that lives inside the dashboard to change the radio station. It did not respond. He repeated himself, raising his voice a few decibels.

"I don't think it's hard of hearing," I offered. "Maybe you used up your three wishes. Or perhaps you should speak to it in its native language."

"I don't speak German," he reminded me.

"Well, can you at least try to feign an accent?" He was not amused.

A few days later, my husband took the car on what he said was a quick errand. When he did not return in a reasonable amount of time, of course I became concerned. I called him, and found out that he had, in fact, been home for over an hour, and was sitting in the driveway trying to establish a verbal rapport with the Mercedes.

I no longer worry, when, after winding up his day's work, he disappears. I know he is safely ensconced in the garage.

I also finally understand why I have been getting so many hang-up calls on my cell phone. I thought I had a secret admirer. But, alas, it was only the car!

It will take some time, but I'm certain that eventually car and driver will develop a harmonious relationship. Hopefully, we can look forward to many more happy, healthy years, top down, riding off into the sunset.

House (Not So) Beautiful

I hope you're not angry with me because I haven't invited you to dinner lately. I'm aware that you have had us to your house a few times, and I have not reciprocated. The truth is, I would love to. But there is a major problem. I no longer have a dining table.

You see, my husband has undertaken the redecoration of our home. In contrast to my affinity for the minimalist, uncluttered look, he seems to favor a very different style. The new decor has a contemporary motif based on two design principles of his own creation:

◊ Principle I: Nature abhors a clean surface.

◊ Principle II: Every electrical outlet must contain at least one, if not two, charger cords.

It is the former that has prevented me from being a gracious hostess.

This aesthetic should not surprise me, however. Over the years, I have visited several of the business offices that my husband has occupied and I have to say he has been very consistent in his design sense. File folders of various sizes and colors can be seen covering his desk, his conference table, and—when space is at a premium—stacks begin to appear on the floor.

Since he has recently declared himself to be "semi-retired," he is inclined to spend part of the week working from home. This calls into question what he will use for work space.

For a while, we tried sharing a room. We installed two desks and hoped for the best. Our hopes were in vain.

My need for peace and quiet directly conflicted with his need to talk on the phone. Sometimes two phones. I often wondered: Was he a lawyer or a bookie?

An amicable separation was in order. I stayed downstairs; he moved upstairs. Since he still had his city office, I got custody of the larger office at home. That seemed fair. At least it did at the time.

So he was kicked upstairs with his lap top, his printer, his iPad, his iPhone, a land line, a file cabinet, office supplies, and an array of colorful file folders. I helped him get organized. This solution seemed rather promising. At first.

Shortly, in an insidious progression, sheets of paper and entire file folders began sneaking out of the file cabinet and onto the dining room table with a proprietary attitude. Noticing me noticing the potential impact this might have on our eating habits, he promised to have them all put away by the end of the day.

Which he did. For a while. And, for a while, I was able to push the remainder aside, and still manage to set two places for dinner.

But did you know that file folders have this nasty way of reproducing? Sort of like rabbits? You can't leave them unsupervised because they begin forming stacks. First they cover the table. Then they move to the top of the buffet. Finally, when you can no longer see the wooden surfaces, they start stacking on the floor. They have begun to look way too familiar!

The files and other assorted papers have now taken up full-time residence in what used to be our dining space. It's been months since I've seen my table. Presently, I'm keeping a very watchful eye on the living room.

I turn now to Principle II, the matter of decorating the electrical outlets.

I have never felt there was anything particularly objectionable about a naked electrical outlet. But, apparently, my spouse does not share that view. Little by little, each socket in my abode is becoming the permanent home of a charger cord.

While I do not deny the ease and convenience of devices such as the smart phone and the tablet, they are hungry little devils and seem to require constant feeding. My husband relies on them heavily, and as a result, has determined that he needs to accommodate their hearty appetites from every room in the house.

Let me further explain that the cords are in residence even when they are not engaged in their designated purpose. This, according to my husband, minimizes the risk of misplacement.

As I write, there are two cords gracing the outlet in our entrance foyer, lying on the floor looking like dormant, anorexic snakes. (One of them actually is for his GPS golf watch, which he uses only on the weekends. Nevertheless, the cord remains *in situ*.)

A long, white cord graces the bedroom night stand. In the living room, two more cords are artfully draped over a formerly lovely piece of sculpture that decorates a counter top. My personal favorite happens to be the one dangling from the outlet in the bathroom.

So now that you understand the situation, I want to add that you are more than welcome to come for dinner. As long as you don't mind sitting with a tray on your lap.

Oh, and if you need to wash your hands in the powder room, check to see that the electrical cord has not landed in the sink—preferably *before* you turn on the water.

DEEP THOUGHTS

Epiphany

I think I have figured out the afterlife.

If I go to heaven I will be surrounded by exquisite delights that are no longer accessible to me here on earth.

For example, for years I enjoyed eating a particular mint candy that, in addition to having just the right amount of zing, also happened to be sugar-free. What a perk for the diet-conscious. Good taste without the calories.

Suddenly, it's gone! I checked out all my former suppliers: the drug store, the supermarket, the convenience store. I was told by all of them that the manufacturer stopped making it. I'm sure there was a good reason. Probably all the toxic chemicals that made it so tasty. But, still…

Then there is my V-8 Juice. I love V-8 Juice, and unlike the sugar-free mints, which were a guilty pleasure, when I drink V-8 Juice I feel like I'm infusing health into my body. So convincing are their commercials.

My V-8 Juice of choice was the one that the label indicated was "calcium enriched." I was excited to be having a tasty drink and at the same time daring osteoporosis to attack me. Slowly, my particular type of V-8 began fading from store shelves. First one supermarket, then another. I finally found a store that still had some and I bought all of the remaining bottles. I'm down to my last one.

I still search for it when I go shopping, ever hopeful it will reappear. I find regular V-8, salt-free V-8, fiber-filled V-8, tangy V-8, not-so-tangy V-8, and V-8 with fruit, but calcium-fortified V-8 remains elusive.

And then there are Mello-Rolls. Whatever happened to Mello-Rolls? They were cylinders of vanilla ice cream wrapped in paper that we carefully placed into the rectangular top of an ice cream cone. I haven't seen those since I was a kid. I miss them.

I could go on. TV shows I loved that are no longer on the air. The car I used to drive, a compact Chevy Corvair convertible, that today would be considered eco-friendly. My favorite shade of lipstick that the manufacturer made a unilateral decision to discontinue. Gone, all gone, but waiting for me in heaven.

I have also imagined hell.

I'm convinced that if you go to hell you are condemned to an afterlife of grating, irritating, obnoxious sounds that constantly call out to you—and you have no choice but to respond. There is no rest. You run from one demanding sound source to another for all eternity.

Beep! Beep! Beep! Beep! Is it your coffee maker? Is it your microwave oven, your dishwasher, or your refrigerator scolding you because someone left the door open? Maybe your washer or dryer, demanding to be emptied, filled, folded? Your electric iron that is ready, or not ready, yelling at you because you have ignored it for too long?

Ring! Whoosh! Clang! Sing! Your cell phone won't take no for an answer. It's smart, smarter than you. It beckons, and like Pavlov's dog, you respond. Phone call, phone message, email, headline, appointment alerts. Two o'clock in the morning. It doesn't care. If you are summoned, you leap out of bed. Your training has been successful.

Turn left! Turn right! Make a U-turn! Don't turn! Your GPS badgers you until you do what it says. This is the part of hell where you ride around and around at the whim of the voice from the dashboard, and never, ever arrive.

So, for the rest of my days here on earth I shall strive to be a good person. Not that I've been a *bad* person, but I will become an even better one. I want to be let into heaven. Once there, I will drive to the store in my white Chevy Corvair with the red leather seats, and I will stock up on sugar-free Mentos, calcium-enriched V-8 Juice, and Mello-Rolls to my heart's content.

Then I will drive home, lie down on a soft, comfy cloud and watch brand-new episodes of *Seinfeld*, *The Guardian*, *Northern Exposure*, *Route 66*, and all three versions of *Law and Order*, on my celestial flat screen TV that doesn't make one single sound. Unless *I* want it to.

Drive-Thru Nation

I noticed something at the last cocktail party I attended (which was also the first cocktail party I have attended in about fifteen years). The guest list was comprised of a mixed crowd consisting of current and former urban dwellers, who, surprisingly, got along quite well, in spite of one group secretly thinking that the other was out of its mind for living in/moving away from "The City."

But I digress. What I noticed was this: the urbanites seemed to feel more comfortable in a vertical position, arms at their sides (unless they were holding a drink) and feet more or less parallel to each other on the ground. In contrast, their country cousins appeared more at home occupying the available chairs (there are never enough chairs for everyone, but I digress again), body at a ninety-degree angle, knees apart, arms slightly extended, with the right foot at least twelve inches ahead of the left foot. I thought this odd at first, until I realized that this was a perfectly natural accommodation to a lifestyle choice: living in the suburbs means living in your car!

I, personally, have experienced the same metamorphosis. After spending the majority of our lives as city people, my husband and I decided to give it all up for the greener, quieter life of a small community. I knew how to drive when I lived in the city, but hardly needed to do it. Since the move, however, my car and I have become co-dependents. At first, I thought this was a bad thing—until I discovered the wonderful, efficient world of drive-through, or as we aficionados efficiently call it, drive-*thru*, a world to which mere pedestrians have no access. Why, just the other day, I completed an entire list of errands without once leaving my auto. I tell you, city people, life does not get any better than this.

My day begins with a run (I now use the term figuratively) to the dry cleaners. From my driver's side window, I peer out at a large stomach and hairy arms as a man without a head (I assume it is a man, due to the hairy arms, but you never really know) accepts my dirty laundry through a slot in his window, and passes me my clean clothes on a hanger, which I then place on the little hook behind me. (Why is there a little hook behind me? Did the car designers anticipate drive-thru?) I pay, receive my change, say thank-you to the non-responsive stomach, and drive on.

Next stop: the drug store. I used to go inside, but no more. I pull right up to that magic window, say my name to a somewhat flatter stomach, and out comes my prescription. Wonderful!

I glance at the seat next me and notice the letters I have to mail. No problem—there's a drive-up mailbox just around the corner. Maneuvering my car just right, I pull up beside it, lower my window, and plop those babies right down the chute. *I'm getting really good at this,* I compliment myself, *better than last time when I didn't get close enough and actually had to undo my seat belt!*

I look at my watch and see that it's time for some mid-morning refreshment. Aha! Starbucks Drive-Thru is just the thing. This is a two-part process. It will be somewhat more challenging, but after the success at the mailbox, I'm up for it. I stop at station one and lower my window. A disembodied voice, encased in considerable static, comes through a little metal box, greets me, and asks for my order. At least, I think that's what he/she said. In any event, I yell out my order, and drive up to station two, where I'm lined up behind three other cars because some #@%#&! driver no doubt ordered six lattes: *Grande, vente,* and whatever, mocha, vanilla, decaf and caf, iced and hot, one pump or two, whipped cream or no. I sit, rapping my fingers on the steering wheel, trying not to be impatient, and tell myself it's a small price to pay for the lack of wear and tear on the soles of my shoes.

And thus, I steer through the rest of my day. The drive-up teller at the bank, a naughty jaunt through McDonald's, a trip through the car wash to get rid of the tell-tale smell of the French fries. And then the library drive-by book drop-off. The satisfaction of accomplishment is more than I can express. It almost cancels my greatest fear: that one day my car windows will get stuck in the closed position and ruin life as I now know it.

The only down side of my day was getting a traffic ticket on my way home. But even the officer told me not to get out of my vehicle.

I believe I have become a drive-thru junkie. I am actually considering a cross-country trip for the singular purpose of visiting those drive-thru joys that I have, to date, just read about and not yet experienced: a drive-thru wedding chapel, confessional, strip club, funeral home, and emergency room!

I am having drive-thru dreams. (Perhaps I need a drive-thru therapist.) The other night, I imagined a drive-thru pick-up window at my grandchildren's pre-school. I drove in, gave their names, opened the back window, and down they came on a slide, right into their car seats. They thought it was great fun and I was not required to sacrifice my ego by having to stand in the waiting area next to those "younger," sexy moms in their workout clothes.

So you see, the world of drive-thru presents endless possibilities. We just have to be creative. If we can think outside the box, we may never have to step outside the car!

Traffic University
(or, Things that Go Bump in the Night)

It's three-thirty in the morning and I'm awake. I'm awake because the dog jumped on me. The dog jumped on me because he's afraid of thunder.

Why was there thunder? The weatherperson didn't say anything about rain in the forecast. I watched the late-night weather and traffic reports, and remember hearing about the broken water pipe that would cause traffic jams during tomorrow's rush hour, but not a word about rain in the middle of the night.

Yet it was unmistakable. There was a thunderclap, causing the dog to jump on me and wake me up. What more proof do I need?

I'm lying on my back, staring upward, and suddenly find myself unable to fall back to sleep because I'm obsessing about the weatherperson. What motivates one to become a weatherperson?

Weatherpeople, like dentists, are not always regarded with affection. They are blamed for spoiling picnics and baseball games. Right now, I'm angry at the weatherperson for not preparing me for the thunderclap in the middle of the night. I might have given my dog a tranquilizer. Then I wouldn't be lying here thinking about how tired

I'm going to be tomorrow. But it's not tomorrow, is it? It's already today. I'm going to be tired *today*.

Weatherpeople have credentials and a fancy title: meteorologists. They should be able to do a better job of predicting. At the moment, the weatherperson is even lower on my list than the dentist.

In a moment of kindness, I try to picture the weatherpeople as children, someone's sons or daughters. Perhaps sweet, nerdy kids with an obsession about barometric pressure, a need to understand Noah and the flood, the source of lightning, or why it hardly ever rains on the Jewish High Holy Days.

Signs of this passion must have been evident in their young lives: a strategically placed autographed photo of Willard Scott, twelve copies of the movie *The Perfect Storm* in the video cabinet, a room decorated with posters of Punxsutawney Phil, a younger brother locked out of the house during a hurricane in order to measure the force of the wind gusts.

These young scientists worked hard, went to college, then graduate school, took courses in physics, chemistry, calculus, and thermodynamics. So when we finally see them smiling at us in front of the weather map, as they explain the cold fronts and warm fronts that only they can observe because of their exclusive Doppler radar (how can they *all* have exclusive Doppler radar?), we should feel a measure of confidence. They have been well educated and are now qualified weather professionals who provide correct predictions at least fifty percent of the time. But not tonight.

This is not helping me. I'm still awake. My thoughts are no longer my own, but are controlled by sleep deprivation. The TV screen in my head is now playing the traffic report. A new obsession takes hold: How does one become qualified to talk about traffic?

Like the meteorologist, does the desire to do this type of work stem from a childhood passion? Did the candidate once delight in setting his Matchbox cars on fire or throwing his toy Hess truck over a cliff? And, if so, is there a program of higher education for future traffic reporters? Is there a degree program in "trafficology?"

Tomorrow—I mean later today—I will begin my research. I intend to call AAA and google traffic schools—not the ones that teach you how to drive, but the ones that teach you how to talk about driving. About accidents, lane closures, and jack-knifed tractor trailers. About demonstrating enthusiasm while reporting a twelve-car pile-up.

A course on discovering alternative routes, or the history of the cloverleaf interchange. A section on how to be constantly, annoyingly perky while delivering all sorts of bad news. Perhaps an elective on selecting outfits that are chic and stylish while also providing ample freedom to point and sweep your arm up and down across a giant road map. (The weatherperson could benefit from this elective, as well. Perhaps it can be an interdisciplinary offering.)

What about flying the helicopter? You know, the traffic helicopter that flies above the interstate during rush hour and shows you how nothing is moving? Maybe we should save that course for graduate school.

I wait for daybreak. There is much to do. My sleepless night has not been in vain. If my idea is implemented, it is sure to mean a brighter future for the educated traffic reporter. And, for all us viewers, we will be able to feel as secure with the advice we receive about the best route to work as we do in the weatherperson's ability to predict a dog-waking thunderstorm in the wee hours of the morning.

The Shape of Things to Come

I am starting to have serious concerns about the survival of our species. There is no reason to believe that humans can last forever with our current anatomical design.

I mean, just consider the dinosaurs. They walked the earth for 150 million years, and might still be around today if they had been willing to grow fur coats to withstand the Ice Age. They have no one to blame but themselves for evolving into nothing more than wire and bones, confined to life in a museum.

Adaptation is key to survival. Species that fail to adapt become extinct. That is why I am proposing some major changes to our current anatomy in order to survive the Technology Age. This needs to happen *now*—before it's too late!

First of all, we need to rethink our thumbs. In their current stubby little form, they've outlived their usefulness.

Thumbs as we know them were fine for our ancestors the monkeys, chimpanzees, and tree-climbing sloths. While they are still useful for grasping, they are completely outdated for texting or tweeting. And what do we do more of today—grasp or text? And when was the last time you climbed a tree?

A short, fat, rounded digit is totally impractical for the speed and accuracy we now require to communicate with each other via smaller and smaller keyboards on personal electronic devices. A longer, thinner, pointier thumb would be so much more efficient. Completely possible. Didn't fins become arms and/or legs as species moved from water to land?

And once we learn how to reconstruct the thumb, I suggest refining the index finger. While it remains useful for pointing, it is not as streamlined as it could be for maximum usage of the iPad keyboard, or for ordering reading material on an e-reader. If you have ever tried to order Stephen King and gotten Martin Luther instead, you know what I mean.

At this point in time, I wouldn't tamper with the middle finger; I think it is still quite functional for its dedicated purpose.

Moving right along, I would like to recommend a third eye to be situated on the top of the head. This is to prevent *homo sapiens* from stepping off curbs into oncoming traffic or falling off subway platforms because their necks are bent. As a result, the two optical orbs we have long relied on for visual cues are now consistently focused downward, staring at iPhones. Or Droids. Or what have you.

Granted, with the advent of the third eye, visits to the ophthalmologist might take a bit longer—and baseball caps would have to be redesigned—but those are small inconveniences when you consider how many accidents could be avoided. I would hate for future species to read that our kind were made extinct due to confrontations with modern predators, like moving vehicles. Or wars brought on by angry groups of people who are constantly bumping into each other.

Also included in my master plan for reconstruction of the human anatomy is a second set of ears. Look in the mirror. There is actually room on each side of the face to place another ear above the one we currently have. Though it might be considered a bit odd-looking at first, it would be a very practical adaptation. We could continue to stuff one set of aural cavities with ear buds, while having the capacity to perceive important environmental sounds, like, say, the person who is shouting at you that you are about to walk into an open manhole.

And while we are on the subject of stuffing small articles into our ear canals, why should we have to spend money on cell phone accessories? Wouldn't it be cool if, when our adult teeth grew in, one of them was blue?

In the process of accommodating a new age, there may be body parts which will fall by the wayside due to disuse. For instance, since social networking does not require actual talking with one another, vocal cords may outlive their function, and, like tail bones, eventually become a vestige of a past life.

However, although I see our newly engineered bodies as a functional improvement, we must be cautious in our expectations. Adaptation is not perfect. Consider that humans have been standing erect for six million years, give or take, and we still suffer from aches and pains because of it. Evolution has failed to perfect the spine. But maybe if we continue to keep our necks bent forward staring at smart phones for hours on end, we may eventually resume the nearly horizontal posture of our ancestors.

Perhaps some problems are best solved by going backwards.

Now Playing at a Theater near You. Maybe.

Do you like movies? Do you like going to the movies, or are you one of those people who prefer sitting on your couch with a Netflix rental or scrolling through the On Demand list for something worth watching? If you are the latter, then don't bother reading any further. You just won't get it.

But if you're like me, and enjoy getting out of the house and—for the price of a senior ticket—watching a good film on a really big screen with Dolby sound, whatever that is, then perhaps you'll share my frustration at not living in a Select City.

November is the time of the year when the movie industry really knows how to amp up the disappointment! They save the best for last, releasing films at the end of the year in order for them to be in the running for the Academy Awards. These are the films with the finest actors and most intriguing stories. We are enticed with advertisements and coming attractions. We react. *Oh! I can't wait. I must see that!* Then you read the bottom line: *Exclusive Engagements* or *Now Playing in Select Cities. Soon to be Released Everywhere—Eventually.*

But we must wait our turn. Our city is not "select" enough.

I wonder, who are the Select Cities and how do you become one? Is there a rotation of some sort? If that is so, then I wish my city would jump on the wheel.

In my mind, I see a bunch of cities sitting in a classroom and the teacher saying, "OK—who wants to be a select city this month?" And the cities all shoot their hands in the air and cry "Ooh! Ooh! Pick me! pick me!" But, unfortunately, there are those bully cities that are larger than the rest, and are capable of intimidation. So the same cities are chosen all the time and the rest of them, the smaller ones, are forced to return home and confront the stigma of their puniness.

I used to live in a Select City. Perhaps the most Select City in the country: New York. Not in the outer boroughs, but right in the heart—Manhattan. Brooklyn and the rest of them don't even count when it comes to theater selection. As a moviegoer, I was spoiled rotten. I just took my Exclusive Engagement status for granted. *Of course*, I would get first crack at a new release. I had no idea that my rights as a citizen would be so compromised when I made the decision to relocate to a town with fewer than eight million people. And to think I gave up a rent-stabilized apartment!

Listen, I'm not saying that small towns don't get any new releases. Why, just the other day I noticed that the latest Pixar feature was playing on at least three screens in our local multiplex. That should satisfy the moving-going crowd ages twelve and under. Or am I overestimating?

Hollywood, there has to be a better way. On the whole, you are known to be a democratic group. On behalf of smaller towns and cities everywhere, I'm asking you to be fair. The locations where you choose to place your best products should not be based on their representation in the electoral college. (Which is thought by many to also be unfair, but that's a topic for another day.)

Perhaps you would consider a lottery of some sort, or a bake-off? Just a couple of ideas off the top of my head. You're the creative guys. I'm sure you can come up with something to level the playing field.

In the meantime, I shall try to be patient and wait for Anthony Hopkins and Helen Mirren to appear in a theater near me. I knew I was being too hasty in giving up that rent-stabilized apartment!

The Eye of the Beholder

Has this ever happened to you? You're in a restaurant. In your line of vision is another table with, let's say, three couples. You unconsciously absorb the physical details of the six well-dressed people who are about to eat their appetizers. You notice the gray hair on the partially bald men, the obviously chemically-treated hair of the women, the flashlights on the iPhones to help illuminate the menu when reading glasses aren't enough. And yes, those are hearing aids snugly tucked behind at least three pairs of ears. Your conclusion? Boy, there are sure a lot of old people in this place!

Adhering to reality for the moment, as painful as that might be, you overhear that the woman on the left is celebrating her birthday tonight. And guess what? She is, in fact, a whole year *younger* than you are. Wow, you think, she should take better care of herself!

The question is, how accurately do we see ourselves? In public places, I frequently find myself scrutinizing people I consider "older," trying to determine their ages. It's funny how I consistently conclude that they must be at least ten years older than I am.

With each passing year, reconciling my chronological age with the "me" that exists inside my head is becoming more and more challenging. The person that lives behind my face cannot possibly be related to that D.O.B. I just wrote down on the intake form at my doctor's office.

While I can't exactly pinpoint during precisely which decade my self-view became arrested, I can assure you that my alter ego is, in fact, still paying full price for a movie ticket. And that lovely twenty-one-year-old woman calling for "Grandma" can't possibly mean me.

Contrary to what you might be thinking, I don't avoid mirrors. That would be difficult, if not impossible. I prefer to confront my reflection, rather than poke myself in the eye with a mascara wand.

But I have discovered a few tricks that I'm happy to pass along:

Be sure to place your mirror away from the possibility of naked sunlight streaming through the window. And never, never make the mistake of looking into a magnified make-up mirror while wearing a pair of reading glasses!

And what about photographs? I will admit that lately I've grown more camera shy. The person living inside my head is not always happy to be mistaken for the woman in the picture. And selfies are definitely out of the question. My arms simply aren't long enough to get the desired effects.

I know that men can have a similar reaction. My husband, for example, is frequently alarmed by his captured image, and can be heard to mutter "Who's that old man?"

And then there's my ninety-one-year-old uncle who stated the other day that his peers "look so old," implying that he didn't see himself that way. Of course, he might be correct. I don't know his friends.

So, do I really want to know how the rest of the world views me, or do I want to continue to exist in the bubble labeled "you're as young as you feel"? After all, except for the forty-five minutes in the morning that it takes me to recover from night-time stiffness, fortunately, I feel pretty good.

The illusion is not fool-proof, however. In spite of my personal inner life, the world continually presents a series of reality checks.

The cashier behind the ticket window never asks me for proof of age when I say "one senior, please." (What can you expect? She's probably only eighteen and everyone over thirty looks old to her!)

Young men have occasionally offered me a seat on a crowded bus. I don't require it, but I accept. Pride is one thing, comfort quite another.

The bagger in the supermarket offers to help me load my cart full of groceries into my car. I flex my muscles and tell him "I'll be fine, thank you." Clearly, he has no clue that he is actually addressing a much younger woman than the one he sees before him.

In spite of considering myself to be a confident woman with real, serious values, I have a sneaky feeling that this duel between perception and reality will go on. And I will continue to derive pleasure and satisfaction to hear from someone who has just learned my age "Oh, I'm shocked. You certainly don't look it!" Proving, once and for all that I'm not like those other guys. You know, the ones in the restaurant.

The Golf Lesson
(or, Lessons from Golf)

I don't mean to deceive. It's not my fault if people assume that I'm athletic. I certainly don't encourage this. I never discuss sports, my scores, or my best game ever. I do not even talk about how my team at camp always won at color war. (That would really be deceitful, since I never went to camp.) So I figure it must have something to do with my appearance. Maybe it's my broad shoulders, my long arms and legs, or my straight posture. And perhaps that perception is fueled by the fact that I used to be tall, at least until my spine began celebrating more birthdays than the rest of me.

The funny thing is, I never thought about athleticism one way or another until I was in my thirties and tried to learn tennis. (Is "athleticism" a word, or have I just elevated "athletics" to the status of a religion or a philosophy?) For the first time, I was made aware that there was actually a right way and a wrong way to achieve a result in a sport. My inability to rise above a minimal level of competence made it quite apparent that I was going the wrong way.

Nothing in my prior history had prepared me for this. Growing up as a city kid, I did what all city kids did. On the pavement of Brooklyn, I jumped rope, played "potsy" (known in more refined circles as "hopscotch"), and rollerskated. At age seven, I learned how to ride a two-wheeler. My pink Spalding ball, pronounced "*Spawldeen*" in Bensonhurst, was always in my pocket, and I could throw and catch as well as any other girl. In fact, I was allowed to join the boys' stick ball games as I was always good for a single or a double.

So at what age did I outgrow my eye-hand coordination? I really couldn't tell you. I just know that it happened.

After my humiliation at tennis, I took a sabbatical of indeterminate length from my athletic career. This decision was definitely a mood lifter. I was learning to embrace my klutzdom, and was successfully dealing with the fact that my upper body and lower body would never be friends, and that the one half would never tell the other half what it was doing.

So you can imagine how I received my husband's suggestion that I learn to play golf. He, who went to camp, and could play a very good game of tennis, had suddenly decided to renew his interest in this other pastime. I tried to hide my inner terror with a smile, as I posed what was, for me, a terse, but very significant question: "Why?"

"It'll be fun," he said. "Something we can do together." He started sharing fantasies of wonderful golf vacations we could take and how this was an activity we could do even when we reached our golden years. *Reached* our golden years? We were already several karats into that journey. Could I dare shatter his dreams and tell him that golf was definitely not on my bucket list?

My reluctance notwithstanding, I signed up for my first lesson. On the morning of, I pulled on a pair of shorts and a shirt with an alligator sitting jauntily upon my left breast. (I had chosen the alligator over the little man with a stick riding horseback.) I looked at myself in the mirror and knew at that moment that, without a doubt, this would be a complete failure. I looked terrible in golf clothes!

Nevertheless, I actually showed up for my appointment with the golf pro. He was cute. This was a good start. He placed a club in my hands and began explaining how to address the ball. By the time he finished locking my fingers, adjusting my shoulders, bending my knees, and tilting my head, I felt like my body was contorted into the most unnatural position I had ever experienced. I no longer cared that he was cute.

I decided then and there that the person who invented golf in all likelihood had had some serious postural deficits and had created a game that compensated for his unusual bearing. And that he did this because none of the other boys wanted him on their rugby team. If only they had been more sympathetic!

Trying to adjust to the appropriate golf stance was one challenge. The other was trying to decode the language, which sounded like English, but made no sense. Did I hear him correctly when he instructed me to put my weight on my front foot? I had a front foot? My dog had a front foot. Two of them, as a matter of fact. And two more in the back. I, on the other hand, had only a left foot and a right foot which were, as far as I knew, still next to each other.

By the end of the hour, I knew precisely what was meant by a golf handicap. This was definitely going to be another uphill struggle. When it came to addressing the ball, I could think only in terms of four-letter words. My poor bruised ego desperately needed some TLC. I had to think of some compensation, something I could do really well. So I went home and took out the vacuum cleaner.

I won't bore you with the details of my subsequent lessons. Suffice it to say, they were not successful, and I happily walked away. Until one day I opened my eyes, and just like Dorothy, found myself in a magical kingdom. It wasn't exactly Oz. This one was called "Florida."

Like the winged monkeys, golf was everywhere. And since I knew I wouldn't be going back to Kansas any time soon, I decided to try again. I did so reluctantly, regarding this decision as a socially acceptable way to express my masochistic tendencies.

Much to my amazement, I found my Wizard. A golf teacher who reached me, and with plain and simple talk, made it all make sense. Well, some semblance of sense, anyway. Golf will never make complete sense.

All of which brings us to today. I actually like golf. Yes, it's shocking, but true. It and I have reached an understanding. I approach it with respect.

For me, achieving the level of precision, control, and concentration that it requires is a rather zen-like experience. My mind needs to be clear of all other thoughts. It's not about competition. It's just about me and that little white ball. Start thinking about what to have for dinner, and I'm toast! The truth is, I'm often toast anyway, in spite of the intensity of my concentration.

I've also learned that golf is very fickle. You can count on nothing. One day, you play really well, and, the next, all you have to show for your trouble is an aching back. But it's the successful days that make you want to return.

I accept that golf is difficult, and that I'll never be really good at it. But that's okay. My ego is a lot tougher now, and my floors a lot dirtier. As long as there are enough accurate shots to compensate for the back pain!

But there is a major factor that continues to detract from my pleasure: I still hate how I look in golf clothes.

Nook, Book, or Kindle?

Once upon a time, not too long ago, there was just The Book. No, not *that* book, but *a* book. You remember. Actual printed pages encased between two covers. And the only decision to be made was whether to buy the hard cover edition or wait for the cheaper, lighter-weight paperback version.

Then along came the e-reader, turning the most authentic of the three R's completely on its head. Actually, it was the only authentic R, "writing" and "'rithmetic" not actually beginning with an R at all.

I, for one, did not immediately embrace this new technology, stubbornly adhering to the belief that books are not supposed to come with batteries and charger cords. But, eventually, I did succumb, and now do most of my reading on an iPad.

But this decision, however convenient, has caused me no small degree of angst. Not unlike the time in seventh grade when I ditched my boyfriend. I have once again abandoned a love object, and caused a major disconnect with my past.

I have always been an avid reader, a lover of stories. Going to the neighborhood library each week and returning home with an armload of books is one of my fondest childhood memories. The day I learned to sign my name and was rewarded with my very own library card was thrilling. A rite of passage that was, at the time, as significant as a first date, but without all the groping.

I miss books. I miss the smell of them, the feel of them, the romance of them. When I was young and finished a book I really enjoyed, I would hug it to my bosom, or the place where my bosom would eventually be (although it took long enough), and maybe even plant a kiss on its little binding. Somehow, my iPad doesn't move me in this direction.

I know that with my use of an e-reader I am participating in the eventual disappearance of the printed page. And all that goes with it.

Rooms that once contained books will be empty. We will have to rethink the den. Book shelves and book cases will become obsolete. Bookends might wind up as relics in the Smithsonian. And unless we find a secondary use, the book mark will share the fate of the dodo bird.

What will happen to autographed copies, first editions, leather bindings, book signings? Will public libraries become dance clubs?

And how can I possibly dog-ear an electronic page? I know, I know. You're not supposed to dog-ear pages in "real" books, either, but it has been my secret little sin— my personal mark on my personal copy of a book I took the time to read.

But while I lament the fate of the book, I have to acknowledge the convenience of the Kindle and all of its kin. And I suppose we can endow the e-reader with a romance of its own.

I find something deliciously surreptitious, even wanton, about buying a book at two in the morning while lying in my bed. It's like have a tryst with Amazon in the middle of the night. And the gratification is accomplished in less than a minute. (There are all kinds of things I can say about that, but I'll take a pass.) Before I can even light up a cigarette, delivery is complete, thanks to *Whispernet*!

Speaking of sweet nothings and the middle of the night, the e-reader is very kind to bedmates. I am able to read into the wee hours without the need of a bed lamp. Lighting my way to the toilet is a secondary benefit. You just have to be sure you can make it back before the thing turns itself off.

I have grown accustomed to awakening at three in the morning and seeing my husband's face glowing in the dark. At first it was a bit startling, him surrounded by a halo. It took a few seconds to realize that we were not, in fact, dead, and it was only the light from his Google reader. Now I find it quite flattering. A little like candlelight. He looks kind of sexy. I am often moved to interrupt his reading.

And e-readers have other advantages. Traveling, of course. No longer needing space in our suitcase for books, we can pack those extra pairs of shoes and still have room for the bounty of an extended shopping spree. Yay, Kindle!

So I continue to deal with the quandary: Book vs. Technology. With so many people buying and using e-books, I know there's no turning back. And I certainly don't want to be a dinosaur. But curling up on the couch with my iPad on a rainy afternoon just isn't the same as holding a book in my hands.

Books are three dimensional. E-readers are flat. To me, it's the difference between having the real object or just a picture of the object.

So next time I want to buy a book, what will I do? I like to think I will follow my romantic attraction to book jackets and trot on over to my local bookstore and plunk down the money for the real McCoy. Unless, of course, the desire overtakes me in the middle of the night, when I will have no choice but to rekindle my affair with Amazon.

The Meaning of Life (Time Warranty)

Come on, admit it. We're all subject to occasional morbid thoughts, especially at that point in life when the number representing our chronological age exceeds the highway speed limit. Don't tell me that you never think about the Grim Reaper, the Dark Angel, or any of the other euphemisms you can name to avoid the "D" word.

I confess to having morbid thoughts on three different occasions during the past month.

Maybe it was prophetic, but what most recently got me thinking about time and mortality was the need for a new watch. An awkward movement of my left elbow while leaning in to apply mascara had landed my old, faithful, *expensive* timepiece on the unforgiving tile floor of the bathroom. Its poor little face was smashed to smithereens, and even with my untrained eye, I knew it was broken beyond repair.

The next day, I called upon my friend, the consummate shopper (every woman knows one), who, of course, directed me to the *absolute best* place to purchase a new watch. As I perused the jewelry case, looking for watches whose numbers could be seen without the aid of reading glasses, I was approached by a salesman who offered to help. He removed several models from the case and laid them before me on the requisite piece of black velvet cloth.

He pointed out the virtues of each model, stopping at one that he declared to be a little more expensive, but which came with a life-time warranty. His comment was the catalyst for Morbid Thought #1: *Whose life-time*, I mused, *mine or the watch's?*

At that precise moment, I happened to glance at another customer who was a least thirty years my junior. Pointing in her direction, I asked the salesman, "See that woman over there? If she buys this watch, does she also get a life-time warranty?"

"She certainly does," he replied as if talking to someone recently declared incompetent.

"Then I should get a discount, shouldn't I?"

"A discount?" he repeated, with an unnecessarily steeply rising inflection.

"Of course," I answered in my best "isn't-it-obvious?" tone of voice. "She is clearly a good deal younger than I. Therefore, her life-time warranty will be in effect much longer than mine, so why should I be charged the same?"

He opened his mouth to speak, but said nothing. I left him to ponder my logic, and decided not to purchase a new watch that day.

Morbid Thought #2, by sheer coincidence, also occurred during a shopping trip, interrupting an otherwise very pleasant afternoon. This time, I was accompanying my husband, who was on a quest to find the perfect sweater. We were in the men's department of a very nice store, and since I knew what he liked, we separated to cover more territory in less time. I wasn't successful, but when I rejoined him, he had found two potential candidates.

Both sweaters were the same style, both flattering colors, both a fine wool. One, however, was significantly more expensive than the other, and therein was the dilemma. Rationalizing the possible expenditure of some extra dollars, he stated that the sweater that cost more would probably last longer.

That's when in happened. I thought, but didn't dare utter: *At our age, can you be sure you'll get your money's worth?*

He must have read my mind, because in the next instant we were walking to the check-out counter with the black cashmere V-neck sporting the lower price tag.

Morbid Thought #3, which was, in reality, a morbid utterance, snuck up on me during the performance of a very ordinary domestic task—replacing a missing button on my husband's shirt. My hand stopped in mid-air as I thought of other small, "maternal" functions I had assumed over the years, such as rethreading the draw string which, for some reason, he was forever dislodging from his sweat pants.

"Honey," I called to him.

He responded on my third attempt to get his attention. "Yes?" he said, as he raised his head from his iPhone.

"I was just thinking," I said, as I lifted the shirt towards him, "in the event that I should pass on before you, would you like me to teach you how to do this?"

He laughed heartily, though I'm not sure at what.

I'm pleased to say that I haven't had another morbid thought in at least a week. Maybe this is predictive of a trend. I hope so. I am, in fact, feeling so optimistic that I went watch shopping again, but to an altogether different store.

The friendly salesman spread out the black velvet cloth, upon which he placed three different models, all fashionable, all with numbers that could be easily read without intense magnification.

"And this one," he said, lifting one of the watches off the cloth, "costs just a little more than the other two, but comes with a twenty-five-year warranty."

" Great," I said. "I'll take it."

LIFE IN THE SLOW LANE

Outliving My Teeth

I had an experience recently which was an eye-opener. Or I should say "mouth-opener," since it concerned a visit to the dentist.

While dental visits are not on my list of top ten earthly delights (I refer you to "Traffic University," above), it was the only way I could think of to get a chronically loose crown reaffixed. All I had at my disposal was Elmer's glue, which—according to the warning label—is for external use only. And I make it a policy never to tamper with warning labels.

"Well," Dr. Painless said, "don't know how long we can keep doing this. You really ought to consider an implant. Or two." He said this as casually as if he was suggesting I purchase a scoop of ice cream, or two, and not something that was going to require a root canal (or two). "And by the way," he added, "when was the last time you had a full set of X-rays?"

Gee, I hadn't exactly entered that information into my diary, so I looked at him dumbly and said, "I really don't know." That was definitely the wrong answer. I should have invented some specific time frame. My failure to do so resulted in consigning my mouth to withstand the pain and suffering of having to bite down on a least a dozen pieces of film framed in cardboard stiff enough to support the roof of a small building.

The target number of X-rays was sixteen, but I informed the clinician after I had endured the first twelve, that there would be no more. I spewed this out with my jaws clenched, lest she try to sneak another one in there if I actually opened my mouth to speak.

Very proud of myself for resisting, I sat in the dental chair enjoying the relief from no longer having sharp cardboard edges digging into my palate. That is, until the dentist reentered, put the developed pictures on the light box, and turned to me with an expression that could not have been more serious if he had been about to announce my imminent demise. He focused my attention on the light box, upon which were my illuminated teeth, roots and all, in various shades of black and white.

I don't know about you, but I find looking at dental X-rays a real turnoff. In general, I prefer to remain unacquainted with non-visible body parts. In fact, now that I've gotten older, I find I would rather ignore even some *visible* body parts. Once, a doctor actually sent me full-color photographs showing the results of my latest colonoscopy. Perhaps if I didn't know what I was looking at I might have found it more aesthetically pleasing, but I doubt it. I mean, really, a nice, non-illustrated letter telling me that everything was fine would have sufficed.

So as I stared at the skeletal images that looked like something out of a horror movie, Dr. P. explained, with the aid of a laser pointer and a professorial voice, that while my teeth were fine, my inner bones were in a tragic state. If I didn't act immediately, I would be at risk for becoming *edentulous*. Several sentences later, I finally figure out that "edentulous" meant that one day I would be toothless! Well, won't we all, if we live long enough?

Dr. P. went on to suggest an emergency appointment with a specialist. I was to leave the realm of the dentist and enter the rarified world of the "-dontist." It was to be my first "-dontal" experience, having been spared the need for an orthodontist when I was a child.

Dutifully, I sat in the plush examination chair in the plush office of the periodontist, listening to him "tsk" and "hmm" as he reviewed my X-rays. I got a sinking feeling that I was about to be asked to contribute financially to my fine surroundings and the half dozen lovely female assistants moving to and fro. He did not disappoint.

The treatment he suggested as a way to prevent further destruction of that which was holding my teeth in place, plus those two dental implants, would come with a hefty price tag. I stared at the "-dontist" as I realized that the cost was way more than the required minimum distribution from my IRA.

I needed some time to think this over. "Can you give me a minute alone with my X-rays?" I implored the good doctor. He complied, saying he understood and would come back in five minutes.

My mind raced through various pathetic scenarios. How much longer did I have before my molar got stuck in a piece of toasted bagel; before my incisor impaled itself on a bite of crisp, juicy apple; before kernels of corn were being scraped off the cob because I could no longer safely gnaw? Wait! I think I just hit on the heart of the matter. Maybe it is simply a matter of time, I tell myself.

The -dontist returns and asks me if I have reached a decision. In the tradition of my ancestors, I respond to his question with a question of my own: "So tell me, doctor, how long do I have?" He looks perplexed. "Before my teeth fall out," I reply. "Five years, ten years?" He says he can't tell me that with any accuracy. He is reluctant to give me even a ball park.

"Why do you ask?" he queries. I fire another question. "Do you know how old I am?" He looks at my chart, and answers, "Yes," he has that information.

"So," I reason, "if my teeth will last another ten years without this expensive treatment, perhaps that is good enough. And if I agree to this expensive treatment, can you give me a guarantee of longevity?"

I knew at a glance that he thought I was being highly unreasonable. And, of course, I was. But I think there comes a time in one's life when it is not inappropriate to measure the risks, discomfort, and costs of one's non-life-threatening condition against, the risks, discomfort, and costs of *treating* the non-life-threatening condition.

In the end, I agreed to the dental work. And I believe it will be worth it. Because now, in addition to the hope that one day my bachelor sons will decide to marry, outlasting my teeth has given me something else to live for.

The Grandkids Are Coming!
The Grandkids Are Coming!

All over south Florida, the cry can be heard. Grandparents everywhere have marked their calendars. It's Presidents' Week, and the children have a school holiday. They will visit, and life as you have come to know it will be suspended for the next five to seven days.

Whether this event makes you feel like Paul Revere or Chicken Little, or perhaps a bit of both, you recognize that the atmosphere becomes charged with anticipation.

In our case, the youngest three of our five beautiful grandchildren, ages five through eight, will be arriving, along with their parents and teenage cousin who will be the mother's helper. A party of six will be sharing our bed and board. How do I explain this to the dogs?

Over time, I have come to regard these visits in phases—three phases, to be exact. There is the pre-visit preparation phase, the "peri-visit" actual time together phase, and the post-visit clean-up phase.

The adrenalin is flowing as I launch into my Phase One checklist. There is much to do. The removable safety fence that surrounds the swimming pool must be reinstalled. It's a two-person job that is guaranteed to trigger an argument between my husband and me concerning the proper installation procedure. Every time we install it, I can't help but wonder if it will be the year that one of us pushes the other into the water. We somehow manage to get it accomplished and remain dry.

I'm on to item two of Phase One: assessing toys and games. Will the bikes we bought them last year be too small? Is the Candyland game too babyish? Am I willing to tolerate Play-Doh? Do I mind if the couch gets covered with the sparkles they like to use for arts and crafts projects? Am I still agile enough to step over giant-sized floor puzzles? Will they be upset that I dismantled the Lego tower that they constructed last year? These are all crucial questions which I need to answer before moving forward through Phase One.

I decide to make a phone call and ask if there is a special toy or game they would like me to have ready for their visit. "No," I politely tell my five-year-old grandson, "I will not get you your own iPad." But I do promise that we will not make him use his big sister's hand-me-down pink bicycle. I ultimately succeed in getting some suggestions we can all live with.

Moving right along to item three. This year we have finally decided to give in to the pleas for a new bed for the guest room. The current bed, we have been told, is old and just not big enough. We go to the local mattress store that advertises on television. I look for the tall, good-looking guy who's in the commercials—the one who owns the company. After all, I figure this is as close as I will get to sharing a mattress with a younger man. I ask for him, but am told that he doesn't actually work on the sales floor. So much for truth in advertising. We buy a bed anyway.

The bigger and better bed requires bigger and better bedding. Another day of shopping results in a new mattress cover, sheets, pillows, blankets, and a duvet. I believe we've just spent the equivalent of first-class air fare to Paris.

And last, but by no means least, there is item four of Phase One: food. We want to avoid the potential of a grandchild meltdown due to the wrong brand of cream cheese. I ask for, and receive, a shopping list. It is two pages long. It is also well-organized and categorized into organic, vegan, and "we'll take our chances." Chocolate yogurt from the Swiss Alps? Too bad we already spent our European airfare on the bed. The nearest organic store is fifteen miles away. No matter—at least it's closer than Switzerland. If this is their hearts' desire, this is what they shall have.

More than an hour of shopping has passed, and I'm still looking for something called "Vegenaise." If I only knew what it was, perhaps I could find it. Since I'm unfamiliar with this store, I've already sought assistance from every employee and am embarrassed to ask again. My husband is growing impatient. I leave without the Vegenaise.

On the drive home, we are stuck in traffic. I become anxious that "Amy's Frozen Strawberry Snack Pockets" and "Uncle Dan's Frozen Chicken Nuggets Breaded with Organic Gluten-Free Flourless Flour" will thaw. Who are Amy and Uncle Dan, anyway? Are they Sara Lee's organic in-laws?

The next day, I repeat the shopping process at my local supermarket, filling in the blanks with those items deemed not pure enough to be sold at the organic store. This is far less humiliating. At least I know where to find the white bread.

Phase One: Preparation is now more or less complete. We are ready.

Our two-car motorcade makes its way to the airport to begin Phase Two: The Visit. We wait in the "Meeters and Greeters" area, along with other eager nanas and papas. We are early and check the "Arrivals" board at two-minute intervals. Finally, we see them. All of the work of Phase One is suddenly so very worth it. The three little ones run to us with outstretched arms.

We wait for the bags and try to use logic on the youngest as to why it's not a good idea to ride on the luggage rack. He complies, but I don't think he's convinced by my logic as much as by my tone.

They ask me if I've bought another puppy so they can each have a dog to walk. I tell them that they will have to continue to share the two we have. They are visibly disappointed. Not a good start.

Once outside, we hold a high-level summit meeting to decide who should ride with whom. "You rode with Grandpa last year," the middle one shouts at the oldest, "so it's my turn now." Is she making this up, or does she really remember that? My money's on the latter. Amazing.

We arrive home and review some house rules. The white couches in the living room are still off limits. Please remember to flush the toilets. And, yes, bugs will fly in if you forget to close the doors.

It is a truly wonderful, active, noisy week. They have all become excellent swimmers. No further need for the pool barrier. They astound me with their prowess as little fingers fly across the keyboards of iPhones. I know that they are just playing video games, but I'm convinced the next step is asking Siri to explain the facts of life.

The bed is a huge success, and I think I'm forgiven for buying the wrong kind of chicken nuggets, and not finding the Vegenaise. I also realize that, except for showing up for his kibble, I haven't seen one of my dogs in five days.

All too soon, Phase Two is over, and the two cars make their way back to the airport. Do I see the older one taking notes on who was sitting where?

Back home, I assess the premises. I'm pleased that the house has survived another visit. It wasn't an invasion by Redcoats, and the sky did not fall.

Time to launch Phase Three: Clean-up. I gather up the wet towels and put them in the laundry room. I think there may be one unused hand towel that my husband and I will have to share for the day's showers. The sheets, however, can wait for tomorrow.

Three days later, the laundry is finished, folded, and replaced on the shelves. The toys have been gathered and put away. Finally convinced that calm has been restored, the missing dog emerges from the closet.

I find a paper airplane in the linen closet, and ponytail holders on the kitchen floor. A little white tee shirt was left behind in the kids' room. I smile as I hold on to each of these souvenirs. We shall miss them until we see them again.

But I don't have too much time for melancholy. According to the school calendar, spring vacation is right around the corner, requiring the re-launching of Phase One as we prepare for the arrival of the next grouping.

Fifty Shades Reconsidered

Two significant events occurred this week:

1. I had another birthday, and
2. I finally read *Fifty Shades of Grey*.

"What is the link between these two seemingly unrelated happenings?" you might ask. Even if you didn't ask, you know I'm about to tell you.

My birthday, of course, forced me to confront the reality of my chronological age. Even more depressing, however, the book forced me to face the possibility that my potential for acting out sexual fantasies may very well be over; novel erotic positions are guaranteed to give me leg cramps.

As I'm sure all of you already know, *Fifty Shades of Grey* is about a kinky relationship between a *very* unreal twenty-seven-year-old drop-dead gorgeous male who is a self-made gazillionaire, and a somewhat unreal, beautiful twenty-one-year-old female recent college graduate—who is still a virgin. She is an English literature major with a perfect grade point average who, nevertheless, expresses her emotional astonishments by repeating the phrases "holy crap," "holy shit," and "holy fuck" on alternating occasions.

In an interview, the author, E. L. James, says she wrote the Grey trilogy—which has been phenomenally successful—in response to her mid-life crisis. Well, what can I say? I am long past that midpoint and still have not written my magnum opus. So I had this idea. Seniors deserve a turn-on they can relate to. I will rewrite *Fifty Shades of Grey* for the geriatric set. I don't like to think of my effort as plagiarism, but more like a *Fifty Shades* franchise.

Since my version will be written for those of a more advanced age, it is both responsible and legally prudent that the book come with a warning: "Opening this cover, or firing up your Kindle, may be hazardous to your health. Consult your physician before reading. Perusing this volume may result in: shortness of breath, atrial and/or ventricular fibrillation, spiking of blood pressure, shingles, varicose veins, loosening of dental implants, and short-circuiting of hearing aids."

All of the above notwithstanding, I offer you my first installment:

Judah Gold, shortened from Goldberg, encounters Anna Steelman at a class reunion taking place in Boca del Mar y Lago, Florida, where the phrase "fifty shades of grey" refers to the hair color of all those in attendance who have given up on the shades of Clairol.

Judah remembers Anna from high school as a pretty cheerleader with sexy legs, whose pom-poms used to give him an erection. He approaches her. "Anna," he calls out, checking the name tag on her left breast just to be certain, casually sweeping his eyes over to her right breast as well. He takes in the rest of her with an appreciative eye, noting that she is still very attractive, and that he finds her love handles a turn-on.

"Holy cow," she says, "Judah Goldberg. I haven't seen you in over forty years." She does not fail to appreciate him as well, noting his still-handsome face, almost full head of hair, trim physique, and expensive clothes. "*If he can still drive at night,*" she muses to herself, "*he would be a perfect catch.*"

"It's Gold now, Anna," he says in a rich, sophisticated voice with just a hint of a Long Island accent, "Judah Gold."

"You look wonderful, Judah," she remarks. "You've kept yourself very fit. Clearly, your Medicare supplement includes the Silver Sneakers program at the gym."

"I have a personal trainer, Anna," he corrects her, somewhat haughtily. "I'm very wealthy."

They chat and catch up on the intervening years. Both are widowed. He informs her that he is retired, and living full time in Boca, except when he uses his private jet to visit exotic locales, or his helicopter to take him shopping in Palm Beach.

"And how are you keeping busy?" she asks.

"I have a new hobby," he replies. "I practice domination."

"Domination?" she repeats querulously. "Is that anything like canasta?"

He is instantly stimulated by her naïveté, and tries to quiet his throbbing prostate. He tells her he will explain in due time, and they continue talking. He is becoming aroused by thoughts of bringing her to his home, where he has turned his Florida room into a tropical pink playground of submission.

By the end of the evening, Judah has asked her out to dinner the following week. Anna's inner *yenta* urges her to accept. Because he wants to sweep her off her feet, he resists inviting her for the early bird special. Although he is wealthy, he is also very frugal when it comes to restaurants.

On the evening of their date, he has his driver, Barber, pick her up at 6:30. Judah is waiting at the restaurant and escorts her to the table. "Sit," he commands her. The waiter brings the menus and Judah orders for both of them. In a short time, the appetizer arrives. "Eat," he tells her. During the meal, Judah's cell phone rings. As he excuses himself and walks away to take the call, he instructs Anna, "Stay."

Why does he talk like a dog trainer? she wonders to herself, but is soon distracted by the delicious food.

Dinner is pleasant, and Anna is becoming giddy from the wine. Judah decides to make his move. At their age, they cannot afford to waste time.

Anna agrees to go to his house for a nightcap, after which Barber will take her home. She is overwhelmed by the size of his estate. "How do you manage to get around all these acres?" she asks him.

"Remember, Anna," he responds, "I'm very wealthy. I have my own golf cart."

Anna "oohs" and "ahs" at his beautiful artwork, the expensive furnishings, the 14K gold grab bars in the bathrooms. He escorts her through all of the rooms but one. He is conniving to make her curious. She takes the bait.

"What's this room?" she asks, glancing at the closed door of the former Florida room.

"That is where I play at domination," he responds in a suddenly curt and clipped manner.

My, thinks Anna, *he certainly is moody. Nothing like my Harry, may he rest in peace.* "So let me see," she implores. "Perhaps it's a game I can teach to the girls at the club."

Again, he finds her naïveté a turn-on, but tells her that before he can show her the room, she has to sign a disclaimer that she is entering at her own risk. She is puzzled, but consents. He produces the paper as she searches through her handbag for her reading glasses.

Once the formality is accomplished, he proceeds to unlock the door. Anna steps inside and gasps. She has never seen anything like it. In the center of the room is an ornate king-sized four-poster bed covered in expensive satin fabric with a palm tree motif. Little monkeys decorate the matching pillow shams. Silk ropes are tied around each of the posts. On one wall, at least twenty very expensive Gucci and Pucci silk scarves are hanging on hooks. She spots a tie rack with clearly very costly men's ties. Another wall contains a rack with canes of various sizes. To the left of the bed is a rhinestone-studded walker. Could those be handcuffs attached to the grip? A wheelchair upholstered in genuine snakeskin, and equipped with restraints, stands by the window. Ropes with leather wrist cuffs hang from the ceiling. *Where am I?* thinks Anna. *Have I stepped into a Neiman Marcus holiday catalog or a rehab center?*

Anna nervously begins biting the knuckle of her right thumb.

A woman biting her right thumb knuckle has always been the sexual tipping point for Judah. He can stand it no longer. He pulls Anna to him. His hands caress her love handles. He kisses her squarely on the mouth, his tongue finding its way between her teeth, as he backs her onto the ornate, king-size four-poster bed.

To be continued…
Maybe…

(I'm working on two chapters of insipid emails between the main characters. In the meantime, watch for the movie, featuring Barbra Streisand playing Anna, showing in only the most select cities!)

Fifty Shades Greyer

When we last left Anna Steelman and Judah Gold (né Goldberg), she had just been introduced to his Florida Room of Pain (a.k.a. "the Pink Playground"), and was being ravished atop the ornate four-poster bed by a turned-on Mr. G. He succeeded in awakening stirrings within her that she had not experienced since discontinuing hormone replacement therapy some twenty-odd years earlier. At first, she confused these sensations with a bladder infection, but soon discovered they were dormant sexual longings.

Anna quickly learned that the game of domination had absolutely nothing whatsoever to do with canasta—possibly strip poker, but definitely not canasta—and that a sub, in this case, was *not* a hero sandwich. Uncertain of her limits, but intrigued in spite of herself, she agreed to become his sexual slave. *After all,* she reasoned, *how far can he go? We're not exactly kids anymore, you know!*

Judah suggested they establish a "safe word" that she could use if he did, in fact, get too frisky due to an extra Viagra. After tossing around several possibilities, like "Uncle" or "Get off me, you sick bastard," they agreed on "*Genug,*" Yiddish for "if you don't stop right now I'll kick you in the *kishkas.*"

Anna also discovered that, in addition to liking kinky sex, Judah was very possessive. He wanted to know where she was and with whom at every moment she was not with him. To this end, he presented her with a laptop computer and a special cell phone so he could call, email, or text her throughout the day. She reluctantly accepted these devices, but absolutely drew the line at wearing an ankle monitor. Her inner yenta was also appalled by this suggestion, reminding Anna that she was prone to fluid retention which often caused swelling in that precise body part.

Anna was not familiar with laptop computers, however, and mistook it for a cutting board. Luckily, her eight-year-old grandson, who happened to be in the kitchen, stopped her just as she was about to chop onions. He then proceeded to teach her how to use it for its intended purpose.

At eleven that evening, Anna was startled awake by a strange dinging sound. Ruling out all other sources—such as maybe she forgot to shut the refrigerator door and all the food was spoiling—she finally realized it was coming from the laptop. Anna opened the cover, releasing the bright light, and, sure enough, there was the first email from Judah.

To: Anna Steelman

Subject: What are you doing and with whom?

Date: April 12, 2012, 23:10:06

Dear Anna,

Sorry if I disturbed you, but I get particularly jealous at night, and need to be reassured that you are alone in your bed.

Sincerely,
Judah Gold, President and CEO, Boca del Mar y Lago
Homeowners Association, Phase I

Oh my, thought Anna, *he* is *crazy*. Nevertheless, she found his jealously exciting, and decided to answer him.

To: Judah Gold
Subject: Take a sleeping pill
Date: April 12, 2012, 23:14:05

Dear Judah:

For this, you wake me up? Although I find your jealousy flattering, may I remind you that my late husband died ten years ago, and except for the dog, who died four years ago, I have been sleeping completely alone. While it is a little lonely, I have actually been sleeping better since no one is snoring in my ear. That would be the dog, not my late husband. So would you please refrain from late night emails. The dinging gave me quite a start.

Sincerely,
Anna Steelman, Treasurer, Women's Canasta Society of Vista Shores

To Anna Steelman
Subject: Sorry about that
Date: April 13, 2012, 9:30:10

Dear Anna:

I'm sorry I disturbed you last night, but it was relieving to learn that you have not replaced your husband or your dog. I hope you have a restful day because I have big plans for us tonight. Later today, Barber will deliver a dress and matching shoes that I bought for you and would like you to wear this evening. And, by the way, do you have a bra without quite so many fasteners? Undoing all those hooks last time inflamed my carpal tunnel syndrome. I can't wait to see you. I'm tingling with anticipation.

Judah Gold, President and CEO, Boca del Mar y Lago Homeowners Association, Phase I

To: Judah Gold
Subject: Tingling
Date: April 13, 2012, 13:20:04

Dear Judah:

Barber just arrived with the dress and shoes, as well as the bra that fastens with Velcro. Sorry you weren't here to see me rolling my eyes when I opened the box. I think you had better take down the tingling a few notches, because I won't be wearing any of it.

First of all, the dress. I can't tell the front from the back. Either way, I haven't worn a neckline that low since my hospital gown fell open when I was having my tonsils removed. I was four at the time.

And the shoes. Judah, do you really want to spend the night in the emergency room watching some teenaged doctor tape up my ankle? I will consider the bra, however. Under the circumstances, Velcro does seem practical.

Anna Steelman, Treasurer, Women's Canasta Society of Vista Shores

To: Anna Steelman
Subject: Our Agreement
Date: April 13, 2012, 14:07:07

Dear Mrs. Steelman:

May I remind you that you agreed, when we were together, that you would wear the clothes I chose? I insist you wear the blue dress. Regarding the shoes, you may have a point there. My itinerary for the evening does not include the emergency room. Barber will come around again with another, lower-heeled version. And, for rolling your eyes, you will be punished!

Laters, baby!
Judah Gold, President and CEO, Boca del Mar y Lago Homeowners Association, Phase 1

To: Judah Gold
Subject: Anger Management
Date: April 13, 2012, 14:30:10

Dear Mr. Gold:

Do I detect anger in your communication? May I remind you that I reserved the right to decline any garment that revealed more skin than would be appropriate at a bar mitzvah party? I don't know what kind of affairs you attend, but if I showed up in the blue dress, the party favor for every child would be a case of PTSD.

Tonight, I shall put on something of my own choosing, but promise to wear the sexy lingerie, even though it makes me feel a little foolish, something like Victoria's Secret meets Depends.

And what, pray tell, do you have in mind for punishment? I can hardly wait. If it's anything like the last time, I better take an extra blood pressure pill. I can't believe what you've awakened in me.

Insatiably yours,
Anna XO
P.S. What's with the "laters"?
Anna Steelman, Treasurer, Women's Canasta Society of Vista Shores

And here we leave Judah Gold and Anna Steelman as their digital footprints continue to trek through cyberspace.

I predict that, eventually, the emails will stop when they move in together. She will give up her smaller space for his lavish house. Having found someone who believes he is a good person and worthy of love, Judah will give up his fetish and allow Anna to turn the Pink Playground back into a Florida Room, where they will spend many happy hours together playing canasta.

Steppin' Out with My Baby

I have mixed feelings about formal occasions. On the one hand, each one is an opportunity to release my inner child and play dress-up. On the other hand, my outer "mature" adult cringes as it contemplates the possible necessity of Spanx or other constricting undergarments. Even the idea of panty hose makes me shudder.

So when the invitation came requesting our attendance at a charity ball as the guests of the honoree, my inclination was to say "No, thank you very much for asking," and send a donation. My life would be no less rich for having missed one more mass-produced meal and some boring speeches. And I could lounge comfortably at home in my finest Russell athletic wear, sans undergarments if I so chose.

But there was a personal connection to the guest of honor, so we accepted. Besides, the venue was enticing. The affair was to be held on the USS *Intrepid*, the WWII aircraft carrier which is now a sea, air, and space museum located on Manhattan's west side. Even if it did not turn out to be entertaining, the evening at least held the prospect of being educational.

A formal event such as the one I am describing, I believe, brings to light yet another significant difference between the sexes. I highly doubt that a man is challenged by the phrase "formal attire." He simply reaches into his closet, unzips the protective garment bag, removes the tuxedo, and hopes that it still fits. Then, because errand running is encoded into female DNA, he simply has to hope that his wife remembered to pick up his pleated shirt from the cleaners after it was last worn.

But a woman, no matter how extensive her wardrobe, will arrive at the inevitable conclusion that she has nothing to wear, despite the perfectly good little black numbers already hanging in her closet. Hence, she must shop for the perfect dress.

This shopping excursion is no mere lark, however. For women of a certain age, it can be a devastating experience. Second only to trying on bathing suits.

Unlike men, who have only to don the equivalent of a school uniform, women are faced with endless choices when it comes to formal attire. Arriving at the best decision requires careful consideration and a frank confrontation with one's anatomy. Which body parts can still be revealed, and which are best left undercover?

Personally, I believe I have surpassed the upper age limit on strapless. But there remains the issue of cleavage. What about sleeve length (be honest, do the upper arms jiggle more now than they did last year)? And hemline—how much leg do I dare to show?

After an agonizing, self-critical afternoon, I purchase yet another short, black, sleeveless cocktail dress. Thankfully, it is not clingy and will require no masochistic undergarments. I have thoughtfully concluded that my knees and upper arms can handle the exposure. I decide to ignore the issue of elbows. I can't see them anyway.

The day of the event, I am gathering my accessories and discover to my horror that I do not own a pair of dressy black shoes. How have I existed without this essential? Clearly, I have to get out more.

I make an emergency trip to a local shoe store. There, I find myself gazing at, not footwear, but weapons! Six-inch stiletto heels attached to a sole and some straps that look like evil props from a James Bond movie. But I know that the only person I would kill with those heels is myself.

"Don't you have a dressy black shoe with a lower heel?" I pathetically ask the clerk. She is smiling, but I know she is thinking that I should try the orthopedic store around the corner. Nevertheless, she wants to be helpful—or at least make her commission—and so she disappears into the mysterious back room where shoe salespeople seem to disappear for all eternity, and finally emerges with two shoe boxes.

She removes the box covers to reveal a pair of silver sandals and a pair of elegant black pumps. I am drawn to the elegant black pumps and am pleased to note they do not have six-inch heels. By comparison, the four-inch heels don't seem that high. In retrospect, I realize that my perception of reality had been seriously altered.

I try on the shoes as cautiously as if they were glass slippers. They are a good fit and hug my feet comfortably. So far, so good. But I have yet to stand.

Slowly and carefully, I rise, hoping that my health insurance card is tucked safely in my wallet. The sensation is vaguely reminiscent of wearing ice skates for the first time and I suddenly want to grab onto a railing. Like a cautious toddler, I take my first step, then another. *Not bad. I can do this.* I'm pleased as I catch a glimpse of my legs in the mirror. Very sexy. Sold!

From the moment I stepped out of the taxi that evening, I knew I had made a terrible mistake. I was yet another victim of fashion. I was afraid to move. I was trapped and terrified. For some reason, strutting around the shoe store and actually walking on pavement were entirely different experiences. Out in the real world, my mobility had been seriously compromised.

Women all around me seemed to be moving with no difficulty on heels even higher than mine. If they could walk without fearing for their lives, why couldn't I? So what if some of them were thirty years younger? I had more experience. I had been walking longer.

I decided that there must have been a balancing technique that they knew and I didn't. So I experimented with various postural adjustments. Holding my shoulders back and thrusting my pelvis forward allowed me at least enough momentum to catch up with my husband, who, bless his heart, seemed unaware that I was no longer at his side.

I immediately linked my arm in his and told him that the only time he could leave me for even one second was when I was safely in a chair.

Did I mention that we were on an air craft carrier? Of course, when I chose these shoes I never considered that we would be navigating the length of three football fields to reach the dining hall. Clinging to my husband, it was indeed the longest trek of my life. I felt as challenged as the man who walked a tightrope across the Grand Canyon. In fact, at that moment, I would have happily traded places with him.

I did not leave my seat once for the entire evening. Dancing was out of the question. As was a seriously needed trip to the ladies' room. I have no idea what we were served for dinner, because I was completely preoccupied with the notion that at the end of the evening, I would have to walk all the way back.

Eventually, the night was over. We thanked our host and I lied as I told him what a lovely evening it had been. After all, it wasn't his fault that I had fallen under the influence of some misogynistic shoe designer.

The shoes came off as soon as we reached the lobby of our building, and I happily walked the corridor with my feet, albeit bare, securely back on the ground. I was still alive. I felt like the winner on *Survivor*.

Note to self: Next time you receive an invitation to a charity ball, send a donation. It's cheaper and much, much safer.

High Maintenance

This will be short and sweet because I have to run off to a doctor's appointment. I don't remember if it's the dermatologist or the ophthalmologist. I'll have to consult my calendar so I don't wind up waiting an hour in the wrong office.

I also have to check my wallet to make sure I replaced my insurance card after the last doctor's visit, and that I have cash, check, or credit card for the co-pay.

Oh, and I'd better verify the status of my underwear, just in case today's appointment turns out to be with the gynecologist.

I used to look forward to the end of summer. I happily anticipated the cooler weather and the fact that my children were returning to school. Now, summer's end has a whole new meaning. It has turned into check-up season.

My car also receives regular check-ups. But I take it to one place and they examine all the moving parts. People, on the other hand, are required to see specialists. Hence, I'm spending the equivalent of an entire month rotating among medical offices.

I don't think it's my imagination, but with every passing year the maintenance list seems to grow longer.

This year I added a retinologist, who, after the exam, suggested I see my ophthalmologist who will, no doubt, send me to an optometrist. Last year, I added a cardiologist. Or was that the year before?

Some visits I don't mind so much. For example, seeing the dermatologist is definitely less stressful than a visit to the gastroenterologist. After all, the only preparation required is that I remove my makeup, rather than the contents of my intestines.

The radiologist's office was kind enough to send me a postcard to remind me it was time for my annual mammogram. I'm not sure whether I will squeeze that in before or immediately after I see the dentist.

I also have a podiatrist on the payroll, but he had his turn last month (during which I did *not* tell him about my new shoes). The periodontist shall have to wait until next month. I would schedule the orthopedist, but he happens to be on vacation.

Don't get me wrong. I'm not complaining, only observing. I'm grateful that, so far, all outcomes have been good. And I shall continue to do what it takes to keep it that way. I just don't understand how someone who feels so young could have body parts that are apparently so old.

Alternate Realities

Even if you are one of those people who claim to be only vaguely interested in television—and swear that you watch only PBS soap operas, British spy movies, The History Channel, or Bloomberg Business—you must be aware when a new season is upon us. I, for one, am an unabashed TV watcher, and I confess this with the same courage with which I own up to my Cool Whip addiction. I do not ask for forgiveness.

As devoted as I am to police dramas, post-mortem dissections, and *Jeopardy!*, I have so far failed to understand the public's attraction to reality TV. I have experienced it at least enough to decide that even five minutes is four minutes too long. If I had watched the Kardashian daughters when I was in my childbearing years, I probably would have run to my ob-gyn demanding to have my tubes tied.

And yet, they return, season after season. Young, well-built, bikini-clad people prancing around a remote island. Young couples jumping out of airplanes and racing around the world looking for clues. Over-dressed bejeweled fashionistas claiming to be housewives—though how they manage to get any vacuuming done between all those cosmetic surgeries is beyond me.

As I am wasting my time pondering why these shows continue to grab the ratings, I review what I have just written. Of course, I can't relate to these programs. Not only is the content totally inane, these people are simply not my demographic. Smarten up, TV executives. There are more than sixty million of us in America over the age of sixty.

And so, in the interest of eliminating age discrimination in primetime TV, I offer an alternative version to one of those mind-numbing sixty-minute time wasters:

The Real Housewives of Century Village

As an answer to *The Real Housewives of Miami*, I offer *The Real Housewives of Century Village*. The stars of the show are six friends of a certain age who reside in a retirement community which, by sheer coincidence, also happens to be located in south Florida.

The group consists of Connie, a platinum blonde; Carole, an ash blonde; Roz, a champagne blonde; and Sue, a golden blonde. Zipporah, playfully referred to by the others as "Zip the Lip," is the token brunette. Jane, the non-conformist of the group, courageously allows her hair to remain its natural gray—although this is subject to change, now that Mr. Lerner, her neighbor, has become available due to the recent death of his wife, may she rest in peace.

Connie, Carole, Jane, and Sue are widows. Roz, however, is recently divorced, her husband having left her for his physical therapist while he was recovering from a knee replacement. After forty-five years of marriage,

Roz bitterly recalls the day she watched him hobble off, leaning on his walker, with his suitcase strapped to his back. Zip the Lip is the only housewife who is still married.

For the first show of the new season, the camera pans in on each of the six *amigas* at home, preparing to meet for a shopping spree at T. J. Maxx.

The first vignette belongs to Roz, who is trying to apply her mascara while weeping over her divorce. She explains to the audience that she still loves him but, at the same time, wishes he was dead. She gets some comfort from the fact that their children are not speaking to him. As she rearranges her champagne-blonde hairdo, Roz tells the viewers that the one good thing that came out of all the intense grief surrounding her divorce was that she lost twenty pounds, and is back to her college weight. She stands up from her vanity to show off her skinny pants with matching jacket from Chico's. She dons the jewelry she recently purchased through binge buying on the Home Shopping Network, and steps outside to the parking lot to meet her friends.

Connie, Carole, Sue, and Jane are introduced consecutively. Connie, who is the most affluent of the friends (her husband owned a chain of funeral homes) walks us through her decorator-appointed condo as she searches for her Bottega Veneta handbag, which, unlike her friend Sue's—she assures us in confidence—is not counterfeit.

We meet Carole, the most indecisive of the group, in her bedroom, still in her bathrobe. Half the contents of her closet are strewn on the floor as she tries to decide what to wear. We politely leave her to resolve her quandary.

Sue has just stepped outside and locked her door as the camera catches up with her. She is a vision in pink with her Chanel jacket and Prada sunglasses. *(But are they?)*

Practical, non-conformist Jane, the only one of the crew wearing sensible shoes, is distracted as she talks to the camera, keeping an eye out for Mr. Lerner, should he emerge from his condo. Her plan is to dash outside and "accidentally" bump into him, offering words of comfort, and a helping of home-cooked brisket. We now understand the purpose of the sneakers, which clearly do not go with her otherwise coordinated attire, complete with dangling earrings.

We are introduced to Zipporah in her kitchen, where she is still yelling at her husband about how he ruined the last night's meal. Fresh from a French cooking class, she was intent on showing off to Connie and Sue, whom she had invited for dinner. But the stupid lout had brought home three cucumbers instead of zucchini squash, completely ruining her plans for ratatouille. Phil is saved from further debasement when Roz knocks on the door to tell Zip that everyone is waiting outside.

During the last half hour of the show, the audience is treated to a discussion about whose car they should use, and who should ride with whom. Carole, of course, is vacillating. Connie and Roz are somewhat on the outs, since Roz accused Connie of cheating at mah-jongg. And Zipporah sullies the air by telling Jane that her dangling earrings make her look like a slut.

Jane still holds a grudge against Sue for sneaking into her bathroom and taking her last Depends, leaving an empty box in the cabinet. Connie is whining because, although she has the largest, most expensive, most comfortable car, it isn't fair that she always drives.

We leave the six friends as they argue in the parking lot.

Previews of the next week's episode invite us to be flies on the wall as the real housewives of Century Village finish their post-shopping spree luncheon, and discuss how to split the check.

I hope this show is a success, because I'm already hard at work revamping other reality series. For example, in my version of *The Amazing Race,* which will be called *I'm Still Walking—That's Amazing,* ten couples compete for a grand prize, which is yet to be determined, but might be a lifetime supply of early bird dinners at the local deli. Considering age limitations and reduced stamina, the playing field will have to be modified, let's say from racing around the world to fast-walking around a gated community, while telling Phil, the host, about their latest maladies.

And my version of *Survivor*? I'm considering an intimate portrait in real time of those facing the challenges of life after being voted off the condo board.

How Old Am I in Dog Years?

They say that, over time, people start to resemble their pets. Or is it the other way around, that over time pets start to resemble their people? ("They" say so many things, who can keep it straight?) I don't know if this adage is necessarily true in my case, but I wouldn't mind if it was. My two dogs are beautiful. On the other hand, I'm not sure how they would feel if they began to resemble me.

While our respective visages may not have merged over the fourteen years we've been together, we have noticeably begun to share other physical changes. For example, my dogs can no longer jump in and out of the back of our SUV, but require a helping boost. While I, myself, have never actually been required to jump in and out of the back of an SUV, I have the equivalent difficulty simply launching myself out of bed each morning. What I am apparently sharing with my beloved pets are all the signs of aging.

Then there is the matter of graying hair. I was able to live comfortably in a state of denial for a long time thanks to chemistry. However, my male dog, Davis—whose coat is golden brown—has, for several years, been sporting a white snout and head, and speckles throughout the rest of his body. He is immediately identifiable as an older dog, and gets such comments as "He looks good for his age." Since I now no longer dye my own hair, I can only hope that that remark could apply equally to both of us.

My female dog, Bette, who is one year younger (or should I say one year "less old"?) than the male, was white to begin with. Therefore, she hasn't suffered the indignity of nature's highlights. However, like me, she does suffer from arthritis. And, like me, this causes her to limp. Her limp is persistent, though, while mine is only occasional. While she walks around looking like she would benefit from a cane, she remains in high spirits and does the best she can. I, on the other hand, have a tendency to whine.

Bette is on medications to relieve her symptoms. One of those medications, which I originally thought was strictly canine, turns out to be the very same drug that a friend of mine takes for his aching back. When the vet told me that I should fill Bette's second prescription at the pharmacy, I was convinced that the art of veterinary healing had really crossed a line.

Off I went to CVS to get my dog some relief, with a prescription that merely indicated my last name.

"Is this for you?" the pharmacy assistant asked, staring at her computer.

"No," I answered, hoping this would go no further. But she continued.

"Patient's first name?" she queried.

"Bette."

"Date of birth?"

I provided my dog's birthday. At this juncture, the pharmacy assistant finally lifted her eyes from the keyboard. She appeared a little startled.

"But that would make her only thirteen years old. How sad that she needs these pills."

"She's a dog," I stated, in my most matter-of-fact manner.

"Oh." She took a moment to ponder this information and then replied, "You know, your insurance won't pay for this."

I acknowledged this unfortunate fact as I took out my credit card.

Oh, and did I mention that Bette also takes a pill to prevent bladder leakage? I suppose an additional tablet is less humiliating than doggie Depends. As for me, I simply try not to sneeze too hard.

I believe my older dog, Davis, has developed a hearing loss. Several years ago, my husband also developed a hearing loss. Repetition of verbal communication has become the norm in my household, if I am to expect any type of response. However, there is a major difference between Davis and my husband. The dog cannot keep saying "What?"

Together, we are experiencing other age-related changes, as well. Climbing stairs has become more of a challenge for them, and may become so for us. Our walks in the park have become shorter and slower due to their diminished endurance. But these strolls are still an anticipated daily pleasure. And, lately, I am finding the shorter duration and more leisurely pace quite compatible with my own preferred tempo.

Their vision is probably not as acute as it once was, but they are not yet bumping into things. And happily, neither am I.

In the park, I watch younger dogs running and chasing balls, and say to my pets, "Remember when you used to do that?" I also watch younger people jogging with ease, and say to myself, "Remember when you used to do that?"

Occasionally, Bette will forget her stiffness as something compels her to break into a run. This lasts for about ten seconds before she slows down again, resumes her hobble, and wears an expression that says "What was I thinking?" I know that feeling. It occurs every time I try to catch a bus.

When we first brought our puppies home, they were much younger than we were. But, as dogs will, they have caught up. They have become our contemporaries, and we, theirs. There is a certain beauty to be found in sharing our "golden" years with them. In many ways, life has taken on a certain mellowing that wasn't there before. And, in the fourteen years we've been together, we have never felt closer.

Recently, Bette has begun laser treatments to relieve her arthritis. The vet suggested that I might try the same.

Going forward, I know that I will agree to any treatment within reason to assure that my dogs are comfortable and maintain any possible residual of their youthful aura. But, love them as I do, if there's an allocation in the budget for cosmetic surgery, that belongs to *me*.

Dinner with Friends

Do you remember when dining out with friends was nothing more than an enjoyable way to spend an evening? When choosing a restaurant depended only on the type of food you preferred to eat that night—and where your table was located may have been a preference, but was not necessarily a dealbreaker? When noise level was not a major consideration, and every few sentences of conversation was not interrupted by someone on the other side of the table saying "What?" When the waiter did not have to repeat the specials three times, and then move around the table, and recite them three times again? When your biggest problem was finding a baby sitter?

Those were the good old days before dinner with friends became a negotiation.

The process still begins with a phone call to make the date. Your friend suggests trying the new Italian restaurant, Cosi Fan Tutte. "Hold on," you say. You check with your husband. He wants to know if it's going to be one of those loud places. You ask your friend. She doesn't know; she hasn't yet been there. You tell him she doesn't know. Next question: Are the waiters real Italians? Your friend asks what difference that makes. Your husband says, "If it's noisy, and they have accents, forget about it!"

Okay. Your friend relents, and suggests you go back to the place where you ate last time. What was it called … the Quilted Alligator? "Honey, how about the Quilted Alligator, again? The waiters are mostly American, except the one from Kazakhstan, and we can try to avoid him." He says that's fine, but he'll only go there if we can get the round table on the right that's up two steps in the other room.

You remind your friend that, before she makes the reservation, she should ask if they changed the light bulb in the chandelier like they promised, so you won't have to bring your flashlight to read the menu.

"What time would you like to go?" your friend asks, starting to sound a bit exhausted. You ask if six-thirty is okay. "Make it seven," she says. She doesn't like to sit with the early birds. She checks with her husband. No later, he says, or else he gets heartburn.

They offer to drive and will pick you up at 6:45. Your friend says not to worry, that her husband has finally gotten some new eyeglasses that do wonders for his night vision. You recall the last time he drove after sundown and you felt lucky to get home alive. You take some comfort in the fact that it's Daylight Saving Time. And if it's really dark on the way home, she always drives.

You think that the plans are finally set when the phone rings again. It's your friend asking if it's okay if the Browns join you for the evening. You call out to your husband to ask if he minds if the Browns meet you at the restaurant. He says that's fine, but only if Mrs. Brown sits on his right side. You want to know why this is important. He reminds you that that's his good ear, and she has a soft voice. You explain this to your friend, who promptly tells you that she didn't mind choosing the restaurant, making the reservation, requesting the table, providing the transportation, and even asking about the light bulb. But she simply refuses to take responsibility for the seating arrangements. You tell her that you understand and that you don't blame her, and decide it's probably not a good idea to remind her that you get a stiff neck if you are seated too close to an air conditioning vent.

When all is said and done, you wonder if making dinner plans is worth it. Restaurants today have changed. They just don't seem to meet the criteria for a comfortable night out any more. You want someplace quiet and well lit, where the room temperature is just right. It should be someplace where the wait staff doesn't speak English as a second language, and the daily specials are printed in big letters right on the menu. Someplace nearby that you can reach on foot so you don't have to drive when it's dark. Perhaps it's best to stay at home and order in. At least until they start serving dinner at the Senior Center.

THE X CHROMOSOME

What Would Jackie O. Wear?

Dear Emily Post:

I am a woman of a certain age—revealing the precise number at this time is not necessary. The mere fact that I remember who you are attests to my longevity.

I know that you do not claim to be a fashion maven, but I'm writing to you because you are the arbiter of all things appropriate—the first lady of good taste. And I need your help. On a daily basis, a dilemma confronts me that is so confounding that, as I ponder it, I find that it has become four o'clock in the afternoon and I am still in my bathrobe. I'm unable to clothe myself because I have become immobilized regarding the selection of the proper vestments. And so, Ms. Post (Is it okay if I refer to you as Ms.?) I turn to you for judgment. Should a seventy-year-old woman wear *jeggings*?

Oh, I forgot. You've been dead since 1960. I probably have to explain what jeggings are. They are a combination of denim jeans and leggings, resulting in a pair of pants that hug the buttocks and the legs and show no mercy, in that they show everything else. I own a pair of jeggings, but so does my seven-year-old granddaughter. I ask you, is this right?

I know what you're thinking. Why do I even consider wearing jeggings at my age? Why? Is it my fault that body parts don't age equally and we are forced to employ distraction? In spite of my years, I still have long, slim legs which the tight pants show off to great advantage, thank you very much! So I don a loose blouse and the skinny jeans and let the outfit speak for me. "Hey, you," it calls out, "don't look there, look here!" But I do have serious doubts about the correctness of my choices.

Another thing, Ms. Post. Is it okay if I still wear a baseball cap to keep the sun off my face? Does one get too old for baseball caps? I can't imagine my mother ever wearing a baseball cap. Probably in your day only baseball players wore baseball caps and real ladies wore fancy straw hats. Well, I do own a fancy straw hat—just one—and about seven different baseball caps. Have I been investing my wardrobe budget unwisely?

Here's something else that troubles me. Is there an age limit for shopping at The Gap? Sorry; forget that one. The Gap didn't open until 1969. But I do have other questions you can answer.

Is it time for sensible shoes? Should I get rid of the high heels, platforms, and gaudy sandals? What is the statute of limitations on sexy footwear?

Am I sacrificing my dignity if I continue to wear large hoop earrings and costume jewelry? Should I be flaunting, instead, dainty diamond studs and a pearl necklace? Are those the more mature choices?

So, Ms. Post, that is my dilemma. I don't know how much longer I can go on like this. Wardrobe insecurity is ruining my life, and my bathrobe. I know you are probably a very busy—if slightly dead—woman, but I hope to hear from you before I'm eighty.

Until then, I fear I will have no choice but to blunder forward for the next decade—jeweled sandals on my feet, gold hoops in my ears, a tee shirt (loose-fitting) bought on sale at The Gap, jeggings on my bottom, and a baseball cap covering the grey hair at the top—and hope for the best.

Out of the Closet

Twice a year I am forced to confront a terrible truth. The catalyst for the reckoning happens to be bi-latitudinal (if there is such a word) living. I migrate, like the birds, south in the winter and north in the summer. Unlike the birds, who seem to have mastered the art of traveling light, I transport boxes and suitcases full of spring-and-summer-weight clothing from one location to the other. The foreplay to the actual packing involves opening the door to the closet, staring at the contents in horror, and saying to myself, "How did I get so much stuff?"

It is in that instant when I must face up to the fact that I am a recreational shopper. Not quite as bad as being a shopaholic, but almost. And... it's a slippery slope.

After all, how many adorable tops or pairs of pants or smart shoes does one person actually need? Did I say "need"? To a recreational shopper, "need" is a four-letter word. As those of us who fall into this category readily recognize, "need" has absolutely nothing to do with shopping.

There was a time when I was concerned that my enjoyment of shopping was some kind of neurotic pleasure-seeking compensation for low self-esteem, or a substitute for never having been breastfed. So I discussed the matter with my therapist. She listened raptly, sitting forward in her chair, as therapists do, staring directly into my eyes, while I was staring at her gorgeous Armani suit. Thankfully, her response to my dilemma was very reassuring. "For you," she said, "shopping is not a neurosis, but a creative outlet." A creative outlet—wow! How could I possibly consider stifling my creative instincts? As much as I was overwhelmed with gratitude, I couldn't help but reflect that in all the months I had been seeing her, she had never worn the same outfit twice. I wondered if she, too, was "one of us."

Creative outlet or not, there is only so much room in my closet and one day it was clear that I had reached the tipping point. I had to issue a restraining order on further purchases and undertake a closet purge. A friend of mine, who shares my artistic burden, suggested that I use her wardrobe consultant, who would come to my house and help me rid myself of the excess. How appropriate, I thought. Since I frequently felt that I was possessed by some kind of fashion devil, what better than a closet exorcist!

So she came and performed her priestly magic. Eight large, black shopping bags (destined for Goodwill) later, my closet was cleansed. I felt cleansed, like I could now exist among the righteous. I stared at empty hangers and a blouse that I hadn't seen in two years. This was how I would live from now on. This was the new minimalist me!

My resolution lasted about three months. Not bad. That was two months, three weeks, and four days longer than any New Year's resolution I had ever made. Then the creative impulse began seeping back in. Slowly, at first, but soon regaining its old intensity. But I was on guard.

I began inventing a set of rules. Buy something new; get rid of something old. Maintain the balance and the empty hangers. This worked for a while, at least until a major sale at Bloomingdale's.

I wonder, am I fighting nature? Is the shopping gene part of female DNA? I don't think that most men feel the same kind of rush as women do when entering the parking lot of an outlet mall. But then, again, I'm not inclined to let out blood-curdling shouts of excitement watching twenty-two men in helmets and shoulder pads come rushing at each other, squabbling over an elliptically shaped leather ball on a cold winter's day.

So the war of the overstuffed closet continues to wage, though periodically I do win a battle.

Even so, I am still overwhelmed by the quantity of stuff that gets packed and shipped to and fro. But I am reaching a new level of acceptance of my tendency towards recreational shopping. After all, my bills get paid at the end of the month and I never buy what I can't afford. And I can always purchase an extra box for packing.

Also, I think I have found a solution to the tenement-like conditions in which my garments sometimes reside. My husband doesn't really need all those suits and jackets, does he?

Tying One on in Paris

I hate packing for a trip. I hate packing for a trip almost as much as I hate preparing for a colonoscopy. It's not so much the physical act of buttoning, folding, and strategically placing my clothes in the suitcase as it is the premeditation. I don't know how it is for men, but for most women with a sizeable wardrobe—and that is most women I know—it is the anguish of decision making.

There is nothing worse than arriving at your destination with an overstuffed suitcase and concluding that everything you brought with you makes you look fat.

On a recent trip to France, though, I finally got it right. Two pairs of black pants, three wrinkle-free (more or less) tops in various shades of gray, one jacket, two pairs of shoes—one sensible pair for walking, the other sexy but treacherous and to be worn only when taxis were involved—and fourteen scarves.

My philosophy was that it was okay to wear the same outfit three days in a row (provided you were careful with the onion soup), just as long as you topped it with the perfect scarf. This was Paris, after all. And there is nothing that says French chic so much as a scarf.

French women have it all wrapped up when it comes to scarves. They could be wearing a pair of jeans from a thrift shop and still look like a fashion spread from *Elle*.

It's all about the magic they perform with those pieces of cloth around their necks. So the question I asked myself was this: Can a Jewish girl from Brooklyn learn to capture some of that *je ne sais quoi*, that careless but gorgeous look of casual elegance? Why not? I was once a Girl Scout. I earned a badge for knot tying.

With unparalleled dedication, I formulated a plan of total immersion, the Rosetta Stone for neckwear. For ten days before my trip, I bought and studied every French fashion magazine I could get my hands on. I watched every video available on Google for instruction in how to tie a scarf. (Did you know that there are at least forty-seven different techniques?)

I learned the difference between the basic loop, the wrap, the twist, the braid, the infinity, the roll, and the love knot. I learned what to do if the scarf had fringes or a border, if it was square or triangular, if it was pashmina or made out of silk. This was much more difficult than the Girl Scout manual.

I was finally ready to put theory into practice. Nervously, I stood before my bathroom mirror with my scarves. I started simply with the "modern one loop." This maneuver requires that you merely lay the scarf over your shoulders and wrap it once around your neck. Forty-five minutes later, I finally figured out how to make sure the two ends come out even. This was disheartening. How long would it take me when I reached the doctoral level and tried the Bunny Ears or the Double Rainbow? At this rate, I would miss my plane.

By the time my day of departure arrived, my confidence level had definitely improved. I now had the ability to create a look with my neckwear that did not by default resemble a *tallis* (for those of you who don't recognize this word, it is your basic Jewish pray shawl), or appear that I was attempting suicide by strangulation. I would not stand out as an American tourist when I hit the streets of Paris, but stride around with the same air of insouciance as a competent Frenchwoman, with my jacket open and my neck artfully wrapped.

You will be happy to know that for the duration of my stay, all went well. Each day, I wore a different scarf and became more daring as my knot tying became more and more complicated. So what if it reached eighty degrees and I was sweating profusely? One must maintain a fashion-first attitude.

Did I say all went well for the duration of my stay? Well, that's true if you don't count the incident at the airport on the day I left the City of Lights. That morning, I had reached the pinnacle of my efforts and succeeded at one last attempt of the most intricate of all scarf-tying patterns in my tutorial: the "double roll loop love knot with French braid." Feeling mighty pleased with myself, I took one last haughty stroll around the block before heading to the airport.

You are familiar with the security procedure that requires the removal of outerwear, including jackets and—of course—scarves? So complicated was this particular pattern that I have to admit I was somewhat less than efficient in undoing it. Although I didn't understand what they were saying, I think I earned the admiration of the two security guards who were sent to help extricate me from my scarf.

On the other hand, the growing line of angry people behind me, cursing in many different languages, and apparently concerned only with getting to their gates on time, clearly had no appreciation for what I had accomplished in the name of fashion.

It's Just a Matter of Time

The other day, I met a friend whom I hadn't seen for a long time.

"So," she asked, "are you still working?"

"No," I answered, "I've recently retired."

"So," she asked again, "how have you been spending your time since you retired?"

She might as well have asked me to explain Einstein's Theory of Relativity because, as I opened my mouth to respond, I found that, in fact, I could not. (Respond, that is.) The truth was that, although the days seemed to be passing quickly, I couldn't account for my time.

This was startling. When I worked and had family responsibilities, I could have told you (although I have no idea why you would have been interested) that I would be grocery shopping on Wednesday at six PM and folding laundry two nights a week at eleven o'clock. In fact, one of the things I promised myself in retirement was that I would never again be folding laundry at eleven o'clock.

So, what was I doing with all the precious time I had been given? I decided to follow myself around for a day and record my activities. I would not be caught again with my mouth agape, unable to respond to a simple query. The next time someone asked me what I did all day, I would be ready.

I gathered a pen and pad of paper and put them on the nightstand so that they would be ready in the morning and went to bed—thrilled with the anticipation of what I would learn in the morning. Perhaps "thrilled" set my expectations a bit high:

6:30 AM – I think I am awake.

7:15 AM – I am now fairly sure that I'm awake and decide to test this hypothesis by actually getting out of bed. Go downstairs to start the coffee and feed the dogs. Dogs are grateful.

7:30–8:00 AM – Spend half hour cleaning coffee grounds out of silverware drawer, into which I accidently dumped the coffee grinder. Not quite as awake as I thought.

8:00–8:30 AM – Prepare breakfast for husband and self and eat without further incident. I think husband is grateful but can't tell for sure; head buried in newspaper.

8:30–9:00 AM – Clean up breakfast dishes, shower, and dress. Can't think of a good reason to apply make-up.

9:00–10:00 AM – Load dogs into car and take them to park for a walk. Very pleasant part of the morning.

10:15 AM – Get laundry started.

10:30 AM – Go to desk and turn on computer. Open the bookkeeping program in order to pay bills. Program does not respond. Call the help line number.

11:00 AM – Continue to listen to horrible music and wait for a representative. A man's voice thanks me for holding and assures me that my call is very important to them, and that it will be answered in the order in which it was received. Ponder why sometimes when you call a large company, a woman's voice assures you that your call is very important to them. Wonder whose voice is more reassuring: a man's or a woman's? Spend about forty-five seconds wondering.

11:30 AM – Finally connect to India. (No wonder it took so long.) My man in Mumbai talks me through steps to fix the problem. Adjust to his accent and ask him to repeat himself only three or four times. He actually sounds very charming. Regret not having applied make-up. Problem can not be fixed. Have to purchase updated version of program. Spend additional time getting my credit card information and installing new program all the way from Mumbai. Am slightly amazed by this fact—would be more amazed if not for time on hold and amount of money spent. Spend additional time downloading old information into new program.

1:00 PM – Am off the phone. Spend next hour finally getting bills paid.

2:00 PM – Feeling hungry, I realize I didn't eat lunch. Also realize I forgot to put laundry into dryer. Move wet laundry to dryer, and begin a new load in washer. Go out to get something to eat.

3:00 PM – Go back to computer and respond to emails.

4:00 PM – Take dogs out for afternoon walk. Start to think about dinner. Stop at supermarket. Dogs remain in car. They don't seem to mind.

5:00 PM – Put second load of laundry into dryer. Feed dogs. Begin to prepare dinner.

6:30 PM – Have dinner, clean up dishes. Decide to go to a movie.

10:00 PM – Get home. Let dogs out before bed. Watch a little TV.

10:45 PM – About to fall asleep, I leap out of bed. Realize I forgot something.

11:00 PM – Fold laundry.

Setting the Standard

Every fall, I celebrate as election day approaches. After that, we can perhaps look forward to some respite before the tiresome political commercials are replaced by equally tiresome holiday commercials. Or perhaps not, since holiday commercials seem to start earlier and earlier each year. Speaking of the election cycle, I almost hate to get into anything political, but I feel that I have to.

I'm calling for *more* government regulation. Stop shouting, women of the Tea Party, and hear me out. There is an industry out there that has a long history of deceptive practices, especially where female consumers are concerned. As such, I am demanding a federal investigation of the villains who size women's clothing, followed by the establishment of some uniform guidelines.

Someone has to take a stand for standardization. For too long, the fashion industry has been playing mind games with our bodies and our self-esteem. For the sake of our mental health—and our constitutionally granted pursuit of happiness—there must be consistency.

It should make no difference into which store I happen to wander, or which brand of clothing I decide to try on. If the size tag has a number on it, and it's my number, that should guarantee that the waistband will close without a struggle, no matter whose dressing room I happen to be in.

It is morally reprehensible that, in the span of an afternoon's shopping trip, it is possible to be a size ".5" in Chico's and a twelve in some fancy designer boutique. (I couldn't possibly have eaten *that* much for lunch! And what is "Size .5," anyway?) It is imperative that we put an end to the pain and suffering caused by these mixed messages!

And what about those garments marked simply "Small," "Medium," or "Large"? There, my friends, lies a vast potential for utter confusion. If, like me, you are a size "Small" at Eileen Fisher, and a "Large" or even "Extra-Large" at Ralph Lauren, you understand. (Of course, my personal familiarity with these labels comes only from discount stores—maybe they're more regulated in the name-brand stores.) And shopping from catalogs? Even worse. What are we supposed to make of the following: "Medium (8-10)"? Doesn't L. L. Bean realize that there is a ten-pound difference between an eight and a ten? And the claim that "One Size Fits All." Really?

Perhaps the biggest offenders of all are the European imports. You know, the beautiful dresses with the mysterious numbers that appear on their size labels, numbers like "40," "42," and "44." They would have us believe that their size forty-two is the equivalent of an American size eight. Give me a break! We all know that fashion houses like Dior and Armani design clothing for tall, thin women without hips. Size eight, indeed!

To rectify this, I attest that a strong government position is required. Possibly even the threat of sanctions against future trade.

And, gentlemen, this is not merely a woman's issue. How often have you tried on a beautiful European shirt that you thought was your size, and were unable to close the button that draws the fabric over your belly? Humiliating, right?

As a nation, we have always strived to protect consumers. Shouldn't we have at least as much government control of garment sizes as, say, the regulation that requires disclosure of the contents of a fast-food burger, or the size of a sugary beverage?

In conclusion, I am appealing to our next president. On day one, before you do or do not repeal national health care, you must sign a bill compelling conformity in the designation of size tags. Perhaps even a constitutional amendment.

(This essay was paid for by The Committee for Truth in Sizing, which approves this message.)

My Life on a Diet

It's Monday morning, and I have declared that I am going on a diet. Again. My weight is starting to climb. Again. I'm sure if I try hard enough, I can identify more evil food items that must never again pass my lips—foods that will join the cadre of those already banished, like pizza, ice cream, deli sandwiches, salty chips, and (*sob!*) Oreo cookies.

Off and on, throughout the years, I have lived on a steady diet of diets. That's what happens when, at some very impressionable age, your baby fat doesn't melt and the boy next door teases you about being chubby. And your doctor (not a pediatrician, because once there was such a thing as a family doctor) is telling you that you are pretty enough to be Miss America, but you would have to lose some weight. That's what happens when your friends have developed waistlines and are wearing skirts with extra-wide leather belts purchased at the trendy shop in Greenwich Village where *everyone* went. *Everyone* except you, because you would prefer not to call attention to your middle.

So, at the age of twelve or thirteen, in response to all this weighty attention, I went on my first diet. I lived for nearly an entire summer on hard-boiled eggs, celery, and saltine crackers, while my friends ate potato knishes from Mrs. Stahl's in Brighton Beach, and bought ice cream pops from the cute boy selling Good Humor. In spite of their gross caloric consumption, they could shamelessly stand erect in their two-piece bathing suits, while I never got off the blanket because lying flat on one's back made one's stomach look thinner. (I did lose weight that summer, and also got a really bad sunburn due to my constant Odalisque-like pose.)

I guess that was a kick start for what was to become a regular pattern for the years that followed. When you are genetically predisposed to carrying around extra pounds, you unfortunately find yourself devoting considerable energy to outsmarting those pesky fat cells that are forever laughing at you from behind your belly button.

You name the diet, and I have tried it. Remember Dr. Stillman and his eight to ten glasses of water diet? That mainly kept me close to home—so I guess it didn't matter how I looked in my swimsuit. He preceded Dr. Atkins, and perhaps even inspired him. Yes, I tried that one, too. On the Stillman diet, you gave up all carbohydrates, including fruits and vegetables. Forget about dessert cravings. The deprivation felt so extreme that I had hallucinations about iceberg lettuce.

I tried Weight Watchers before the points, and I've tried Weight Watchers after the points. Weight Watchers after the points is somewhat more challenging due to the arithmetic. Want to know about the grapefruit diet, the cabbage soup diet, or the three-day diet? Just ask me. Celebrity diets? Oprah and Kirstie and I have been up and down the scale together.

I happen to have a personal fondness for the "geography" diets like the Hollywood Diet and the South Beach Diet, and if I add my own hard-boiled egg and saltines regimen, the Bensonhurst Diet. Wouldn't it be great if every state had its own diet? How about the Idaho Potato Diet? Or the Alaska Grizzly Bear Diet?

I actually did well on Florida's South Beach Diet, if you don't count the morning I fainted from lack of sugar while adhering to the Phase One food plan.

But I have reached a time in my life when I am finally asking "When?" When will the extra five pounds stop being a determining force in how I live my life? Or the extra seven or eight? Ten is my absolute limit.

When will I tune out Dr. Oz and his miracle berries guaranteed to speed up my metabolism or his appetite suppressant made from the bark of an exotic tree in the rainforest—although I have noticed that people living along the Amazon tend to be rather thin?

When will I light a funeral pyre for my bathroom scale and perhaps even my full-length mirror, and send them ablaze into the waters? When is that magic age of acceptance when I will finally be comfortable in my own slightly excessive skin?

I hope it happens soon, and I hope—in solidarity with all of my other diet plans—it is on a Monday.

Hair: A Hate Story

Do you want an accurate weather forecast? Just ask a woman. As a gender, we are natural-born meteorologists. And we do it without any fancy equipment or any years of schooling. No need for Doppler radar, barometers, hygrometers, or weather satellites. All we have to do is step outside, remain there for less than a minute, come back inside, look in a mirror, and observe the state of our hair.

For example, we can provide a humidity reading within a fraction of a percentage point by noting if our coiffe frizzes or goes flat. Temperature is accurately predicted by determining the perspiration factor and how it affects our bangs. Rain is definitely on the way if we decide it's hopeless, yank it back with a hair tie, and/ or don a baseball cap.

I have come to believe that most women have a weird relationship with their locks. For one thing, we are never satisfied. If our hair is straight, we wish it were curly; if it's curly we wish it were straight. We change the color and we are forever changing the style. We will pay the equivalent of a month's worth of groceries and fly halfway across the country for the perfect haircut.

For me, personally, I can measure my years as a long string of bad hair days. For the first few months of my life,

I was completely bald. I have photos, lovingly snapped by my father, to attest to this. I'm not sure what they fed me, but by the time I started kindergarten, I had an unruly mess of thick, wavy, curly tresses. At that juncture, the standard remark from the very same loving father was "Susan, you need a haircut." And he no longer took my picture. Thus began a lifelong battle to tame my mane.

In my younger days, my hair grew past my shoulders, and my mother braided it to keep it confined. But how long could a girl tolerate looking like a brunette version of Heidi?

When I got a bit older, we cut it short, which resulted in me locking myself in the bathroom, sobbing uncontrollably, and wondering if somehow I could figure out a way to have the hairdresser arrested. I subsequently destroyed every copy of my sixth grade graduation picture.

By high school, bangs and pony tails were all the rage. That is, *straight* bangs and pony tails, not pony tails that bunched out instead of hanging gracefully down one's back, and bangs that were slick and did not resemble a slalom run as they coursed down one's forehead. It seemed that all the popular girls had straight hair. So I did the math. Straight hair equals popularity. With my mop I would never make it to *American Bandstand*.

So what did us mop-heads do? We weren't going to take this lying down. In fact, lying down became a bit of a challenge as each night before bed we wound our hair tightly around giant mutant rollers. The hope was that in the morning we would awaken slick and tidy. Ever try to sleep with large plastic objects affixed to your skull? I swear, if the CIA had thought of this, there would have been no need for water boarding.

Giant rollers weren't the only self-inflicted torture. We also laid out our tresses on ironing boards and attacked them with hot irons. What we got for our trouble, in addition to hair that stayed straight for maybe ten minutes, was singed ends and an odor that stayed with you all day that was reminiscent of a freshly plucked chicken.

Ever try Scotch-taping your hair to your skin to keep it straight ? I don't recommend it, unless you're one of those people who enjoy ripping off Band-aids.

All of these, of course, were only temporary measures. By the end of gym class, Mother Nature always reclaimed her birthright. And we could not convince my best friend's father, who was a doctor, to write a note excusing us from physical education because perspiration made our hair curly.

I hated my hair throughout the 1960s, when hippie hair was all the rage. The perfect hippie hair was parted in the middle and pony tails were let loose to let hair hang limply past one's shoulders. Somehow, curly hair could never achieve the limp look. I, of course, wanted the limp look. I wish I could recoup some of the hours I spent in the bathroom with a brush and a hair dryer, winding, stretching, and blow-drying until my arms ached.

I would go to the hairdresser (I have since forgiven my hairdresser—are they still called hairdressers?) with pictures cut from magazines of beautiful, sleek hair styles, and I would implore him to make me look like this or that. He would turn away and giggle, then turn back and patiently explain that he couldn't. Not with my hair.

Abandoning everything I had tried in high school, I took the next step. When I was in my late twenties I had my hair chemically straightened. This was serious stuff—stuff that left small burns on my scalp. Who cared? They would heal. And I finally got what I always wanted—the stick-straight tresses of my dreams.

At last, my hair could blow alluringly, like ribbons in the wind, as I rode happily along in a convertible. So what if I didn't own a convertible, or know anyone who did? It was all about the concept. My long, straight pony tail, sticking out of the hole in the rear of my baseball cap, could swing provocatively across my back as I jogged. (I don't remember, *did* I jog?) I no longer had to fear steam rooms. (I could still hate steam rooms, but at least I didn't have to fear them.) Oh, if only those popular girls could see me!

I engaged in this masochistic scalp-burning behavior for several years, until, one day, the Afro hit it big, and fashion gave me permission to go natural. Curly hair was in and straight-haired women were actually getting perms. *Hah!*

For a happy instant I rode the top of the fashion wave—excuse the pun—and was freed from the obsession of having to look like a cheerleader. Unfortunately, however, this did not last. Sleekness made a comeback.

I'm not sure exactly when or how I concluded that if I cut my hair really, really short I could be rid of the heartbreak of humidity. And, once done, there would be no turning back—I knew I would finally be happy. This was to be a great liberation—as good as abandoning the girdle or burning a bra.

Again, I marched to the hairdresser with a photo. I stuck it in his face, and said, "Here, make me look like this!" He seemed a bit stunned at first, but when his speech returned he asked me if I was absolutely certain that I wanted to look like Sinead O'Conner. I reconsidered, and we compromised.

To this day, I am unfailingly punctual about my visits to the hairdresser. It's probably another obsession, but, for me, a better one than uncurling. So attuned am I to the length of my hair, or lack thereof, that when it reaches a certain point I could swear I hear it growing. Now I'm the one who says, "I need a haircut," which brings about a fit of laughter from my husband, and anyone else who happens to overhear me.

I actually get compliments on my hairdo. People ask me if I did it because my head has such a nice shape, or that I knew it would look this good. I simply smile, and thank them.

How can I explain that, after years of irreconcilable differences, it was all about revenge?

Temporary Insanity

No one has ever accused me of being a fanatical housekeeper. On the *Good Housekeeping* scale of good housekeeping, with zero being first cousin to a Collyer brother, and 10 being genetically linked to Mommy Dearest, I would fall somewhere around a 6.75.

The truth is, I'm comfortable with a certain amount of clutter. And, for better or worse, I've learned to live with dog hair. But there are a few occasions during the course of the year when I am completely overtaken by a kind of domestic lunacy.

It has nothing to do with the full moon, and is certainly no longer attributable to PMS—I haven't been able to use that excuse in about twenty years. I'm not sure you'll find the syndrome written up in the medical journals, though perhaps it should be. Since it is without an official psychiatric label, I will refer to it as "relocation madness."

It is as predictable as the changing of the seasons. In fact, it is the changing of the seasons that brings it on. It is the anticipation of our semi-annual treks up and down the east coast that brings on an irrational compulsion to leave the house in such a state of perfection that it appears no one has ever lived there. Not ourselves, not our family, not friends, not two hairy dogs—no one! Household chores that have been neglected for the past six months suddenly take on a sense of urgency. For some bizarre reason, my orderliness standards for vacating my house seem to be higher than when I actually live there.

I no longer try to fight this compulsion. It's hopeless. It's been going on for years. Yoga and meditation have not been successful in keeping it at bay. So I succumb, knowing it will run its course. Under the circumstances, it seems like the only rational thing to do—though "rational" might be a bit generous.

About a week before the designated move date, I awake one morning with a foreboding that I now recognize as the precursor to the malady, sort of like the scratchy throat that precedes a cold. I think it only fair to warn my husband, since, for the next seven days, he will be dealing with my evil—yet very clean—twin. I have long since given up trying to engage him in the process. He just can't seem to get worked up over such things as the organization of the hangers in the guest room closet.

"Starting today, I'm getting the crazies," I tell him as we are lying in bed.

"What are you talking about?" he queries. How quickly he forgets. And it's been only seven months since the last attack.

"It's time to start packing up the house."

He is silent, but I note that underneath his golf tan, he has become quite pale.

A couple of days later, I am still reasonably under control and we have managed to get our clothes sorted, packed, and shipped. Each season I vow to minimize the amount of *stuff* I send off to UPS, but I just know that the shoes I decide to leave behind are the precise pair that I am sure I cannot live without. So, of course, I pack them. Along with everything else that I cannot live without.

"Okay," my husband says, "that's done. Now can you try to relax?"

Relax? He is so clueless. There is still so much to do.

In the middle of the night, he wanders downstairs to find me in the kitchen.

"It's three in the morning. What are you doing?"

"Have you seen the mess in the container cabinet?"

"What's the container cabinet?"

"You know, the place where I store the plastics for leftovers."

"So what's the emergency?"

"The tops and the bottoms don't match." He doesn't understand how I can't possibly leave them in that condition.

"What difference does it make? We're leaving. Who's going to see them?"

"I don't know. The alarm might go off. The police might come. This might be the first place they look."

How can I explain that it's no different than when your mother told you always to wear clean underwear just in case you were in an accident? It's all about other people's perceptions.

I'm on a roll. The next day, I refuse to have lunch with him because I have to reorganize the junk drawer. "It's a junk drawer," he says, "it's supposed to be junky." But there are degrees of junkiness, and this one has reached the doctoral level.

After the junk drawer, I tackle the silverware drawer, making sure that no teaspoon has gotten mixed in with the soup spoons and that all the salad forks are facing in the same direction.

He proceeds to go to lunch on his own and is unfortunate enough to return just as I'm about to begin my next activity. "Get undressed," I order. His eyes shine with a hopeful look. "No," I say, "not that. I'm about to start a load of laundry."

It is our last night in the house. I have finally completed everything to my satisfaction and have come to bed. Suddenly, I bolt upright.

"What is it, now?" my husband asks, not in the kindest of tones as I have just awakened him.

"I have to go downstairs to the laundry room."

"Why?" he asks, which I admit is not an unreasonable question.

"I left lint in the dryer. I can't go off with lint in the dryer." I realize, as I speak those words, that I have reached the pinnacle of my craziness.

We're up early the next morning to lock up the house and leave for the airport. I lie back in the taxi and sigh. I am finally calm. Due to my hard work, the spoons are nesting perfectly, the dining room chairs are in precise alignment, everything in the house that could possibly be washed has been washed. The guest rooms look positively inviting, there is not one single crumb in the food pantry, and the clothes and shoes that we have left behind are as neatly displayed as if they were in a department store.

Although my husband will never understand it, I have learned that there is a certain satisfaction in returning to a place that is perfectly clean and tidy. When I return in six months, I will forget that it was my insanity that accomplished it in the first place. And, in that glorious instant, it won't even matter that within moments the plastic containers will once again be mismatched.

Withering Heights

Once upon a time there was a girl, who, at the age of thirteen, had reached her adult height of five-feet-six-and-a-half inches. She imagined that she towered over her friends, who at that point in time, had reached only five-feet-two or -three. As a result, she felt BIG. Perhaps not as big as Gulliver surrounded by Lilliputians, but at least as big as a horse in a herd of ponies, or a bass fiddle among cellos.

BIG was not a good thing to be at her age. Standing last in line with the one or two other "tall" girls was one thing, but being behind the boys made her feel as awkward as Wilt Chamberlin at a little people's convention. When they palled around with the boys, her friends looked cute. She did not look cute. She was too tall to be cute. But cute was what she wanted to be. She hated her height.

Fortunately, as the girl emerged from her self-loathing early teen years, she learned to embrace her vertical dimension. She gave up her round-shouldered posture in favor of erectness. Her height gave her confidence, a certain strength. Now she was glad not to be one of the petite girls. (Not that there's anything wrong with being petite. Some of her best friends … .) She no longer considered "cute" complimentary when applied to her. In fact, she wished she could be taller, maybe five-feet-eight or -nine. She wore high heels (in those days she could wear high heels without a fear of falling over), and no longer minded if she was taller than her male companions.

She worshipped statuesque women. She idolized Judith Jameson and longed to become her, or some other majestically tall and graceful African woman with close-cropped hair. But, genetically, all she could manage was the close-cropped hair—and maybe a tan.

The girl, now a woman, eventually crossed that point of no return called middle-age. In order to ensure an ongoing state of wellness, physical check-ups became a required annual event. She had learned to fast for two days before appointments to lessen the devastation of confronting the number on the scale, which had a nasty habit of increasing each year. And the nurse had an equally nasty habit of weighing her before she took her clothes off. (She made a mental note not to get her exams in the winter.)

Height measurement? Never gave it a second thought. That is, until the year that same nurse told her she was five-feet-five. "No, I'm not," she responded with an air of indignation. "I'm at least five-six."

"Sorry, dear," the nurse said, "like the scale, the ruler doesn't lie."

Fast forward to the present. Obviously, the girl in the fairy tale is yours truly. Now well past middle age, unless the life span increases to one hundred forty years, I have become victim to that malevolent force that each year causes a person's weight to go up and height to go down. But where are the inches going? I haven't had to shorten my pants or my skirts, so I'm fairly confident that my legs aren't shrinking. Therefore, it must be that my torso is disappearing; you know, that space between the breast and the hips. If this trend continues, will my boobs one day be resting on my waist?

Like Jonah or Job, I wonder if I have been visited with a biblical punishment for being a whiny teen or an adult with too much tall pride. Or is it simply time compressing my spine? Does it matter? I am doomed to spending my last years looking up at my granddaughters.

Having my height measurement taken each year has given a new meaning to the term "acrophobia." Is there no way to reverse this trend? I suspect that Martha Stewart has the recipe for Alice's magical "Eat Me" cake. I will inquire. But, wait … Is it my imagination, or is Martha also looking shorter these days?

I know that the secret to successful aging is accommodation, so I will adapt. I will learn to be happy with my new, smaller stature. I will avoid standing near tall women. But I warn you, when I'm ninety, if I hear one person say, "Look at that little old lady. Isn't she cute?" I will lift my walker and beat them over the head. Or whatever body part I can reach.

Chemical Dependency

I have a healthy relationship with food. I'm neither too thin nor too fat. I eat only when I'm hungry and try not to snack between meals. I believe I am what I eat. I eat this and not that. I heed the media medics. I know that the wrong foods can cause brain shrinkage and heaven knows I need every cell I can hang on to. I'm a believer. I drank the Kool-Aid—oops—I mean the green tea.

I spend an inordinate amount of time in the supermarket reading labels. I've even purchased a pair of extra-strong reading glasses so I can see the fine print. Gone are the days when I would speed-shop through a superstore and, in less than an hour, purchase a week's worth of groceries for a family of four. Six, if you included the dogs.

I sometimes think about the damage my reckless shopping habits might have caused my young family. In retrospect, I can't help but wonder if my son might have gotten into Harvard had I not let him eat all those SpaghettiOs. But there's no point looking back.

Now, as a consumer educated to the perils that lurk on the food store shelves, I devote an entire morning to food shopping for just my husband and myself. And the dogs—but that's a story for another day.

Simple purchases are no longer simple and often require visits to not one store, but several different stores. Take, for example, ketchup. *Ketchup!* What could be more basic in the kitchen than a bottle of ketchup? *Aha!* That was before we knew the potential evils of high fructose corn syrup, one of its key ingredients. Even after I explained the risks of obesity, diabetes, and heart disease, my husband was not happy with the suggestion that he try mustard on his hamburger. Locating organic ketchup was the only way to save the Sunday barbecue.

In the produce section, I look for super foods. I pay attention to their countries of origin. I have even memorized the list of the "Dirty Dozen," which instructs me which fruits and vegetables must have an organic label. I keep a cheat sheet in my wallet in the event of a senior moment. I'm currently working on memorizing the "Clean 15" list so that I can save money by not needing to buy organic, and at the same time learn which foods will not necessarily ruin my sex life.

I buy only organic meat, poultry, fish, and dairy. We now only eat free-range animals that have led a happy, antibiotic-free life, scratching contently in the dirt for their feed, or lazily munching grass in a pastoral field. I prefer to picture them living that way before they sacrificed themselves to my dinner table.

By the time I'm ready for the checkout line, my shopping cart is brimming with super foods. Once again, I can pass the inspection of the food police. Or can I?

If you dig below the surface, underneath the kale, blueberries, pomegranates, wild salmon, and avocado, right down to the bottom of the cart, you will find my secret addiction. That which I cannot live without, and stubbornly refuse to yield. There, under the blanket of anti-oxidants, hides the plastic container of Cool Whip.

No, I haven't failed to read the label. Yes, Cool Whip might well be the epitome of a chemically engineered food. Can I even call it a food when its only nutritionally valuable ingredient is water? Whatever it is, it is my addiction. My guilty pleasure.

Cool Whip has its virtues. It is less fattening than whipped cream, and twice as sensual. Its soft, white, creamy texture evokes thoughts of running naked through a field of cannoli. And the flavor? High fructose corn syrup never tasted so good!

I love Cool Whip on ice cream or frozen yogurt. I love Cool Whip on berries and tell myself that the healing powers of the little fruit will counteract the chemicals. A banana dipped in Cool Whip? Yum!

I eat Cool Whip with cookies and with pretzels, its sweet taste beautifully complementing the salt. It makes a great topping for puddings, and goes well with chocolate—dark chocolate, obviously, because it's "healthy."

Cool Whip goes well with cakes and pies. And, ultimately, I think Cool Whip is delicious all alone, as I swipe my tongue caressingly along the remains on a teaspoon.

I have to admit that my habit has been a bit embarrassing. I keep the Cool Whip hidden in the back of the refrigerator, behind a large container of organic milk. Up until now, no one but my family knew about my addiction. And, bless them, they have been very tolerant, only occasionally reminding me that I was eating poison.

Yes, I know that my Cool Whip cravings are a violation of my commitment to healthy eating. I've thought about giving it up. If I go cold turkey today, I wonder how many years that would add to my life? Can the media doctors tell me? I think I'll text Dr. Nancy Snyderman and put it to her. But until I get a definitive response, pass me that plastic container, please.

The Color Purple?

If decisions I've made in my life were sorted into folders, this most recent choice would definitely be filed away under the heading "What Was I Thinking?" It certainly would not be the only item in that file, just the latest. In fact, if I reflect on many of the decisions I've made in the past, that would be one chubby file folder.

This most recent questionable decision had its origins in what is, for me, a religious activity—getting a haircut. If you have already read about my tumultuous relationship with my crowning glory (see "Hair: a Hate Story"), you know that I have a very short 'do. I get it cut once a month, without fail, and barely make it into the fourth week.

In any event, on one particular day, a little shy of New Year's Eve, I remarked to the stylist how—although it is trouble-free—I sometimes become bored with my look. There is not much you can do with hair that is less than a quarter-inch long. You can't curl it. (Not that I would want to.) A pony tail is out of the question. And hair ornaments don't stand a chance.

"Have you ever considered applying a glaze?" she asked.

A glaze? I had no idea what that was. The word itself evoked associations with Dunkin' Donuts or Benjamin Moore, but nothing to do with hair.

As a graduate of the school of "there are no stupid questions," I risked asking, " What's that?"

She went on to explain that a glaze is a temporary color, not as intense as a dye or a bleach, and that, in time, it washes out.

Okay, then. This was starting to sound interesting. Maybe this was what I needed to perk up my image. "Bring it on!" I boldly declared.

Without missing a beat, she presented me with a color card. "Which one would you like?" she innocently asked.

I gasped as I look down at my choices. Blue, purple, pink, green. Was I choosing a hair color or an upholstery fabric?

Noting my confusion, bordering on horror, she offered "I think you'd look very good in blue. It would match your eyes." How could I explain that nowhere in my wildest dreams had I ever considered color-coordinating my hair with my eyes? So maybe I should go with purple?

Regaining my sanity, I told myself that it wasn't too late to back out. Admitting that I had changed my mind was still an option. The reality was that purple hair did not go all that well with my lifestyle.

"But where is your sense of fun?" said the devil sitting on my left shoulder. "Don't be an old fart. After all, it's almost New Year's Eve. Do something daring!"

Before I knew it, the words were out of my mouth. "Okay, let's go for it!"

Fifteen minutes later, for that's all it took to transform me into something akin to geriatric punk, I was receiving admiring looks and comments from the other hair dressers. "It's great," one of them said, while another one gushed," It looks so-o-o-o-o good on you!"

At this point, my stylist spun my chair 180 degrees so I was finally facing the mirror. OMG! My hair really was purple. Not solid purple, but definitely purple. All I could think was "Please, someone shoot me right now!"

Too bad it wasn't Halloween when my excuse could be that I was appearing as a giant eggplant. Or almost Purim, since I've always wanted to dress up as a prune hamantasch.

My first instinct was to reach for the baseball cap I had stowed in my hand bag for just this purpose. Or, I could ask her to shave my head. Or I could spend the next thirty days locked in my shower with a bottle of cheap shampoo that did not promise to keep your chemically altered hair color from fading.

Or, maybe I would quit the golf club and go to work in a trendy art gallery. Perhaps even consider adding body piercings and a tattoo to complete the look.

But I did none of these things. I left the salon and simply went about my business, with my uncovered head on full display, bearing the occasional glances of strangers as the price I had to pay for my indiscretion. Not quite as shameful as a scarlet letter, but close.

I have to say that my husband was kind. My friends were kind. "It's definitely purple," was all they said. No one questioned my testamentary capacity—at least not to my face.

I'm now a little more than two weeks into my little Technicolor adventure. The purple has faded somewhat, but not completely. In a certain light, it's not very noticeable. But a bright, sunny Florida day still remains highly illuminating.

Would I do it again? Probably not. But it hasn't been all bad. I have had some fun with it. And I've even enjoyed the challenge of coordinating my clothing and make-up to accompany a shade that looks like it belongs in a box of Crayolas.

So, to the people who ask why I did it in the first place, I can only respond with the punch line of an old joke, the contents of which I no longer remember: It was New Year's Eve, and it seemed like a good idea at the time.

VINTAGE WHINE

A Blog About A Blog
(How It All Began)

(With apologies to WordPress, who really were very helpful.)

I wasn't exactly born yesterday. But perhaps in this case, that was the problem. If, like the millenials, I had started out in life texting, I might have avoided all of the trouble in which I found myself over something as basic as changing my mind. When I decided to start the blog that became this book, little did I know that a seemingly simple request for a new title would result in an extended demonstration of just how little I understood technology.

Dear Unknown Blog Support Person:

I am following the help desk instructions on your website, so here is my question. I started a blog with you and now want to change the name of the blog and corresponding web address. How do I do this?

Susan

(Immediate response)

Do-Not-Reply email response:

Dear Susan:

Your question is coming to us through cyberspace as we write and will be answered by one of our friendly customer support people as soon as possible. We maintain control and you must wait your turn. Any attempt on your part to respond to this email may result in permanent banishment from our website.

(Three days later)

Hi, Susan:

So—you want to change the name of your blog, do you? We hate people who can't stick to a decision. Before I bother with you, let me be clear. You want to change both the blog *and* the domain URL?

Marvin V., Happiness Engineer

Dear Marvin:

Thank you for your response. But I need some clarification. Is "domain URL" the same as the "web address?" If so, then yes.

Thank you,
Susan

(Two days later)

Hi Illiterate One:

I can't believe you even asked me that. What planet do you live on? Yes, they are the same. Can we please proceed now?

Marvin V., Happiness Engineer

Sorry, Marvin.
OK, I'm ready.
Susan

(Three days later)

Hi, Susan:

Pay attention. Here are the simple steps you need to achieve your goal:

1. Go to the Dashboard. Press Settings. Scroll down to "I changed my mind."

2. At "I changed my mind" hit "Domain Administration." Look for a little circle. Put a black dot in the little circle and enter your new information.

Is this easy enough for you?

Marvin V., Happiness Engineer

Dear Marvin:
What's a Dashboard?

(Three days later)

Susan–

You are really trying my patience. The Dashboard is what we call our control panel. From there, you can manipulate your blog in any number of ways.

Marvin V., Happiness Engineer

Dear Marvin:

Then why call it a Dashboard? Why not call it a Control Panel? Wouldn't that be easier to understand?

(Two days later)

Susan–

Are you trying to put me out of a job? If we used words that everyone could understand, then we wouldn't be having this correspondence, would we?

Marvin V., Happiness Engineer

Dear Marvin:

Did not mean to threaten you with unemployment. I was just asking!

OK. I followed steps one and two but did not see a little circle in which to put a black dot. I'm sure if I could find the little circle, the rest would all fall into place. Can you help me find the little circle?

(Two days later)

Susan–

The circle is just where I said it is. Maybe you need stronger glasses. In the event that you still cannot see the circle, try these steps:

1. Go back to Dashboard. (You remember what the Dashboard is, don't you?) Scroll down to "I can't find little circle." Hit enter.
2. You will see a list of choices. Go to number 3: Select another geometric pattern. Choose the one that suits you.
3. When you have made this choice, the pattern you selected should replace the circle.
4. Now go back to original location on the Dashboard. You should be able to put the little dot in whatever shape you chose.
5. Insert the new information.

Good luck.

A Blog About A Blog (How It All Began)

Marvin V., Happiness Engineer

Dear Marvin:

You will be pleased to know that I had much better luck with the triangle. However, I still cannot access my new blog with the new web address, or as you call it, the Domain URL. (See, I remembered.)

What do you think the problem could be? I'm growing very frustrated.

(Three days later)

Susan–

You're frustrated? Imagine how I feel. If you can't access your new blog, have you considered replacing your computer?

Marvin V., Happiness Engineer

Dear Marvin:

Please, for both our sakes, is there someone I can talk to? I have a feeling this could all be resolved in a five-minute phone conversation. So far, this has taken almost three weeks and my blog is still not functioning.

Marvin, darling, listen. I'm an "older" person. I'm not that familiar with all the terms and functions.

Don't you have a senior citizen hotline? If you don't, you should.

(Three days later)

Dear Susan:

Marvin has quit. I'm Dave, your new Happiness Engineer. I'm here to help you. Please explain your problem so we can begin.

Trashing My Friends

The holiday season has been over for approximately a month now, and even the slowest among us has probably put away the last celebratory vestiges. Christmas lights and tree decorations have been replaced in their cotton-lined cartons, safely stowed away for another year. Dried-out evergreens have been carted away by the garbage trucks and the fallen pine needles swept into the trash bins. Wrapping paper and ribbon that wasn't decimated by greedy hands has been put into drawers to be recycled for future gift giving. The last of the sour egg nog has long since been poured down the drain, and the dreaded fruit cake pulverized in the waste disposal. Mothers and daughters have begun to take to the malls in droves, January sale shopping being the best antidote for post-yule depression.

While I don't actually share these specific end-of-holiday rituals with my Christian friends—except for the one about going to the mall—the celebration of Chanukah (or Hanukkah if you've never learned to gargle) leaves its own detritus. For example, there is the issue of ridding your kitchen of the lingering odor of fried potato latkes. This can take about two weeks, and a gross of air freshener. In the end, I'm never sure what's actually more desirable: eau d'used canola oil or a freshener called "Southern Magnolia Bouquet."

Then there's the labor of picking the hardened wax from the menorah, the candle holder which burns a total of forty-four candles over the eight nights of the holiday. I can recall a time when picking at candle wax was a sensual experience, but that was from a chianti bottle over a romantic dinner in an intimate Italian bistro. And I was in my twenties. This is as far from sensual as a root canal. Would manufacturing dripless Chanukah candles be a blasphemy against the Maccabees? I guess tradition is tradition, so I spend an entire morning standing over the sink armed with as many small, sharp objects as I can find, and jab at the little candle holders until they are empty and ready to embrace next year's lights.

So Frosty the Snowman melts away in the eighty-degree Florida heat and his song can no longer be heard every time I walk into CVS, and the store where I buy my dog food stops playing "O Holy Night." On the surface, it appears that time has indeed moved on. But one lingering holiday-related issue remains, at least for me: what to do with the greeting cards that contain the beautiful smiling faces of my friends and their families?

These are not like the Hallmark variety of pre-written cards, or the greeting cards from your dry cleaner or newspaper delivery man. Those you might save for a few days and then guiltlessly abandon to the recycle bin. But the family photo cards? I debate their fate as I look through the small stack still remaining on my kitchen counter.

Why, it must have cost the Clarks a small fortune to assemble all twenty-eight children, grandchildren, and dogs in the Australian outback. Not to mention the cost of the photographer. And look at them, how lovely and happy they are, with their healthy, white teeth displayed for the camera. What do I… ? How can I… ? But, on the other hand, do I really want a family portrait of the Clarks in my permanent photo collection?

And here are the smiling Bensons. Not quite as many as the Clarks, but lovely all the same. Oh—look, Tracy's holding the new baby. How sweet! Can I even consider recycling that new baby?

Underneath the Bensons are the Berkowitzes. *Berkowitz*? Why did they do a Christmas card? There are enough people in this group to qualify as a tribe. And Papa Berkowitz did not fail to include his annual family update letter, with each person discussed cross-referenced with the photo. Now I understand the little numbers on their chests. Boy, he really put a lot of effort into this one. So how can I… ?

And then there's Betty. She has no children, but look at her adorable dogs. I do love dogs. I would never trash a dog. But yet…

Here's the next one. They look familiar. Oh, they're my grandchildren. Not the best picture, and I have so many others. Would they forgive me if … ?

So here I stand by the garbage pail, with the photo cards in hand, immobilized by agonizing indecision.

It would be perfect if the cards could self-destruct forty-eight hours after New Year's Day. Until such time as science catches up with need, next year, when you send the new family portraits, may I please request that you include an expiration date?

A Tale of Too Many Choices

Should entering a store to purchase an ordinary item cause an otherwise smart, level-headed woman to put her therapist on speed dial? I didn't think so. Yet I fear I'm in persistent danger of falling into a retail-induced catatonic state, brought on by daily confrontation with really difficult choices. This just might be the worst of times.

I became acutely aware of the situation the other day when I was in Grand Central Station with some time to kill before boarding my train. Needing a new mascara, I entered a trendy cosmetics store. Wherever it was that they displayed the magic wands, I couldn't find them. So I approached a young saleswoman, whose back was to me. I could see that she was deeply preoccupied with rearranging the little eye shadow cases. I realized that this could take a while because she was only up to the naturals, and still had the earth, sea, sky, plant life, and heavy metal color palettes to organize. But I had a train to catch. "Ahem," I said, followed by "excuse me," and then a deep cough. She finally turned and I found myself looking into a face that might have been a display for one of everything they sold in the store, perfectly applied.

"Yes?" she said coolly. "Can I help you?"

I explained that I was looking for a mascara. Here comes the good part. She pointed to a small area on the wall that I had missed, and asked in perfect innocence, "What would you like it to do?"

What would I like it to do? I surely was not prepared for that one. What I wanted to say was "How about making me twenty years younger and ten pounds lighter?" Instead, I said deferentially, "What do you mean?"

"Well," she exhaled. "Do you want it to make your lashes fuller, to separate, to lengthen, or to curl? Do you want it to last for twenty-four hours, or only twelve, to be waterproof, tear-proof, or not run when you open the oven door and steam hits your face?"

"Do you have one that does everything?" I timidly asked, aware that the timbre of my voice now resembled that of a scared eight-year-old. I could tell she wanted to roll her eyes at me, but, to her credit, she refrained, and simply said, "No."

"I'll have to think about this," I told her. I thanked her and fled from the store, completely overwhelmed. I couldn't make a decision of this caliber in thirty seconds; I had a train to catch.

After the mascara experience, I suddenly realized with great alarm that everywhere I turned I was being forced to make similar decisions. For example, have you gone into a drug store lately? Let's start with the vitamins. My favorite multi sits on a shelf at the pharmacy as part of a corps of supplements. There's a bottle exclusively for men, another one just for women. At least that choice is easy. There is a vitamin fortified to help my brain, another to help my heart, and yet another to ensure my bones stay strong. We're not done yet. There's a bottle that will give me extra energy, and finally, the one to take if I'm pregnant. (Elimination of that one from my list is easy, too.)

I stand and stare in horror, realizing that I'm being asked to sacrifice body parts. If I fortify my brain, am I not caring for my heart? As a result, will I be smart, but dead? What if my heart stays strong but I don't know it because my brain is shot? Do I help my bones at the risk of being tired? What good are strong bones if I'm too tired to do anything? Like the mascara, there is no one vitamin that does everything. So maybe I buy them all and take them home and cut them into little pieces and paste them into one pill that will solve all my problems. I search for my therapist's number in my cell phone as I experience the catatonia descending.

Move on over to the toothpaste aisle. Immediately I must decide if I want to fight cavities or prevent gingivitis. Am I concerned about sensitivity? What about the one that's infused with seaweed to provide me with good breath? I'm afraid of that one; I think I break out in hives from seaweed. Shall I whiten and brighten, or reduce plaque? Which one do most dentists recommend? And, yes, I want a winning smile. Of course I do. Who wouldn't? But which one? Why are there so many different tubes of my favorite brand all competing with each other to provide me with oral health and well-being? My finger is now on the button of my speed dial.

And the drug store is nothing compared to the hellish experience of entering a supermarket. My last visit was tragically aborted due to delirium brought on by laundry detergent. I stared at the extended families of liquid soap, not to mention the powders, and they stared back at me, each promising the best possible outcome for all my washday needs. Each swore that it was gentle enough for my delicates, and strong enough for my husband's work clothes. Well, not *my* husband's, exactly. Tax lawyers don't get their suits too dirty. But you get the concept. Do I want whiter whites, brighter colors, bleach or no bleach, scent or no scent, hypoallergenic detergent, detergent for softness, pill prevention, stain fighting, low suds, or high suds? The words flew at me like the pack of cards in *Alice in Wonderland*. "Hello, Dr. Mittman?"

And don't think for one moment that finally making a choice is the end of it. Consider the breakfast cereals. What if I make the wrong choice? What if I fail myself, or even worse, my entire family? I shudder to think of the consequences. I wonder, does Medicare cover treatment for buyer's remorse?

Maybe I'm suffering from retail fatigue, but I long for a time when making an everyday purchase did not conjure up images of *Sophie's Choice*. Perhaps somewhere there is an old-fashioned general store where there is only one type of toothpaste on the shelf, one kind of food supplement, and one, maybe two, laundry soaps. And if I desire to curl my lashes, a jar of petroleum jelly would have to suffice. I don't know about you, but right now it sounds to me like that could be the best of times!

Habits and Other Pastimes

Oh no! Did I just say that? I can't believe I just said that. But I know I said it because I heard myself. The auditory center in my brain is the expert witness. But another part of my brain, the part that hovers over the top of my head and monitors me from outside myself, is in shock.

Of course, you have no idea what I'm talking about. You've come into the middle of a conversation. So for you to fully appreciate my dismay, let me backtrack.

It was early Wednesday morning. My husband had been up and working for at least an hour before I finally conceded to wakefulness, an act which I try to postpone for as long as possible. I went to seek him out. He was cheerful. I generally hate people who are cheerful in the morning, but for him I make another concession.

"I'm ready for coffee," he said. Then he asked me if I would like to go out for breakfast. And that's when it happened.

"But it's Wednesday," I said. "We never go out for breakfast on Wednesday."

This was no insignificant statement, but cause for serious concern. Did my response indicate another giant step towards the porch and the rocking chair? Had I demonstrated a characteristic commonly attributed to *old* people? Was I presently in grave danger of becoming—*gulp!*—*set in my ways?*

You see, the pattern of our life has evolved so that we typically treat ourselves to breakfast at the diner on Fridays. So to be thrown off kilter by the suggestion that we partake of pancakes outside of the house on a different day was a sure sign of impending senescence.

Before my last birthday, would I have picked up on his radical suggestion that we go out for breakfast on a Wednesday and simply said "sure"? Had I crossed some arbitrary line where adhering to a regular routine was more rewarding than spontaneity? Was I becoming inflexible? A person driven by habit? Did I no longer embrace change? Or was I simply overreacting to an innocuous response emanating from an early morning foggy brain?

The latter explanation seems by far the most comforting. For now, I'll stick with that one.

But even if none of the above is true, the very concept of becoming "set in one's ways" warrants considerable reflection.

I began to wonder about other habituated behaviors I might have developed over recent years, and how they might impact my decision-making.

For instance, I realized that I always do my laundry on Thursday morning. So what if my best friend suddenly phoned and told me she had just won a trip for two to Paris on a game show and that she would like to invite me as her companion, but we had to leave right away. Would I say, "I can't. It's Thursday, and I'm about to put the clothes in the dryer"?

Would I really give up a trip to Paris because of a pile of wet socks and underwear? What an absurd question, almost as absurd as this example. No. Of course not. Probably not. Well, I don't think I would.

As I pondered the implications and ramifications of leading a fixed lifestyle, such as foregoing travel for laundry detergent, I recalled an incident that occurred several years ago involving my elderly aunt.

She lived in Florida; I still lived in New York. I had the occasion to be in her neck of the woods and I contacted her without a whole lot of prior notice. I hadn't seen her in a while, and I wanted to take her to lunch. The only day I could make this happen was a Friday.

Even though the invitation was last minute, I thought she'd be delighted to see me, her favorite niece. Instead, she said "Thank you, dear, but I couldn't possibly. Friday is the day I wash my hair."

Shoot me if I ever get like that, I remember thinking. So how do I feel about it now, when I might actually be facing those gun barrels?

When people are described as being "set in their ways" it is usually not meant kindly. On the other hand, what's so wrong about being set in your ways? Is it really inherently bad? What's the matter with having a routine and liking it?

Perhaps one of the perks of getting older is the privilege of arranging life the way I prefer to live it. There are no longer children to rush off to school, or a desk to report to at a certain hour. The structure of my life has become more or less of my own making.

So I ask again: What's wrong about being set in my ways if they are *my* ways? I've had sufficient opportunity to figure out what works for me and what doesn't—what pleases me and what doesn't. So, to the extent that I can be in control of my days, I've earned it!

Therefore, I will continue to do the wash on Thursday and eat bagels only on Sunday. I will continue to crawl into bed at 10PM on most nights and watch an hour of TV before I read myself to sleep. These harmless little traits don't make me intractable, but simply comfortable.

And, in spite of my campaign to remove the stigma from routine, I like to think that I will happily accept a last-minute dinner invitation even if I have just defrosted a pound of chop meat, or be willing to try Netflix, though it took me a year to master the DVR.

May I never become that old dog who can't learn a new trick. Shoot me if I ever get like that.

How I Spent My Summer Vacation

Winter in Florida is not without its benefits, but each May I look forward to returning to the Northeast. So, a few years ago, it was with considerable delight that I anticipated my few months in Connecticut. Little did I know that the summer of 2012 would pit woman against nature and I would become an unwilling extra in a summer that could have been scripted by Alfred Hitchcock.

It all started early one morning. The sky had just become light when my husband was perturbed enough to risk awakening me. "Listen," he asked, "do you hear it?"

"This better be good," I responded.

He said "I hear a rapping and a tapping."

"You woke me up to recite *The Raven*?"

"No, there's a noise, like someone tapping with a hammer." I hadn't heard the rapping, but the insistent sound that came next was my car alarm.

I was out of bed and down the stairs to get a good look at whatever it was that had disturbed my vehicle—and my sleep. Imagine my shock when I spied the granddaddy of all woodpeckers pecking away at my Toyota. *This cannot have a good result*, I told myself, and began banging on the window to frighten him away. "Take thy form from off my car," I yelled at the bird, in my best Edgar Allen Poe. He flew away, but unfortunately, did not quoth "Nevermore."

Later that day, as I embarked on my endless list of errands, I glanced at my left side-view mirror, and to my utter astonishment, it was cracked to pieces. That deranged bird! He had been pecking away at his own image!

Fast-forward to $200 later, a new piece of glass, and utter disbelief on the part of the serviceman who fixed it.

Now fast-forward to two days later, when I entered my car only to find the same mirror cracked again. Obviously, mad Woody had not heard the adage about lightning, and had struck twice. "You had better cover those mirrors," the serviceman said when I told him to order another piece of glass. And, no, there was no discount for two purchases in the same week.

It was an expensive lesson, but for the rest of the summer I compulsively folded in my side-view mirrors every night, and warned anyone who parked in my driveway to do the same. Management took no responsibility for mirrors that were stationary. I don't know what became of Woody after that, although I did hear a rumor about the mysterious breakage of a neighbor's picture window.

So pumped was I by my success in foiling the crazy red bird that I decided to take on the squatter sparrows. There were four of them—two couples who had built nests on either side of my deck awning, under the safety of the eaves. Out of respect for the circle of life—and although I was getting a terrible sunburn—I didn't dream of lowering the awning and disturbing the prenatal activities of the females. What's the inconvenience of bird poop all over my chair cushions when compared to bringing fledglings into the world? And so what if speaking over their chatter caused us to have to shout? I even named them. The couple on the right were Lucy and Ricky; the couple on the left, Fred and Ethel.

But May turned into June, June became July, and still the birds were there. The babies, if there had been any, must have been long gone, but still the parents remained, causing my entire deck to become uninhabitable for humans. Enough was enough. It was time for the Ricardos and the Mertzes to move on. I was cancelling their show. Armed with cleaning equipment and thick rubber gloves, I set out to dismantle the nests and reclaim my territory.

But, like the swallows to Capistrano—or the woodpecker to my car mirror—the sparrows returned.

I caught all four of them rebuilding. Twigs, grasses, feathers, and, of course, more poop were everywhere. I needed professional help. The man in the hardware store sold me a giant roll of mesh netting which he advised I place over the spots where they build. Never underestimate sparrows. They just incorporated the netting into their nests and went on building.

The lady at the Audubon Society suggested shiny Mylar balloons. She assured me that birds were afraid of shiny objects. So I hung balloons and ribbon from my awning. But these sparrows had obviously sought treatment for their phobia.

A naturalist friend advised me to hang small stuffed animals from the awning so the birds would think that predators were lurking. By now, I was so desperate that

I stole teddy bears from my grandchildren when they were at camp, and strung them up by their necks. As a result, besides looking like a bird sanctuary, my deck now resembled a birthday party for the Addams family.

So went the rest of the summer. The birds constructed and I destructed. My obsession was to stay one step ahead. I'm pleased to report that I finally won, sort of. They had found another construction site. But as I still washed bird poop off my windows on a regular basis, I could tell they were nearby, conspiring with the woodpecker, and patiently waiting for me to let my guard down.

New Car Blues

It isn't every day that I buy a new automobile. Therefore, it should be an occasion marked with at least some measure of anticipation and excitement as I drive the shiny, as yet undented, chariot off the dealer's lot. So why, when I should be so happy, do I feel like I want to go directly home, cover the mirrors in my house, and sit on a hard wooden box for a week?

Yes, I am in mourning for my old car, which didn't exactly die, but was economically disposed of as a trade-in for a newer, more fuel-efficient, somewhat smaller version of itself. I had convinced myself that its time had come and that I needed to let it go before it became unreliable. The decision was buoyed by my adult children—who are secure in the knowledge that, being of a certain age themselves, they now know what's best for me. They couldn't quite understand how their mother could care so little for her safety that she didn't have a back-up camera in her car. They didn't understand how I could have craned my neck for years, and only occasionally have stone walls make contact with my rear end.

So who was this person that was shedding tears as she was cleaning out the old car? Do I know her? It is so uncharacteristic of her to become attached to an inanimate object. The person I know considers it a religious experience to make frequent trips to the local dump for the purpose of purging one's environment of "stuff." Yet here she was, crying over a rusting, twelve-year-old vehicle that had clocked enough mileage to warrant a parking space in an assisted living facility.

It just isn't easy separating from an old friend, even if that friend is made of steel and weighs over three tons.

How can you *not* get sentimental over something that has been with you through certain significant events in your life? If you read the old parking stickers on the bumper and window, they could tell the story of homes formerly owned and places formerly lived—a whole jumble of memories.

Open the back and you would see a coating of fur, along with other evidence of two large dogs which this car had transported not just from one place to another, but from puppyhood to old age.

I'm sure if I looked between the cracks in the back seat I would find cookie crumbs and broken bits of pretzels from where my three youngest grandchildren sat lined up in their car seats. This won't happen in the new car—it isn't big enough. And they've outgrown the need for car seats.

The old car was the pair of shoes, which—although scuffed—were perfectly broken in. It was the favorite sweater with the hole in the elbow with which I couldn't part—and if the hole got bigger, or another hole appeared, the initial damage was already done so it no longer mattered.

It was a cocoon, a room of my own on wheels where I felt relaxed as I ran my errands, listened to audio books, and was soothed by the company of my two Labs, who were always eager to go for a ride.

Okay. I'm done now. Thanks for listening.

I don't mean to appear ungrateful. I very much appreciate the fact that I can afford to buy a new car. And the new car is rather pretty, with the romantic-sounding name of "Venza," evocative of some hill town in Italy, although it probably means something quite different in Japanese. I don't even want to guess.

And the new car is trying very hard to make me happy. It does many things that my old car could never dream of doing. It starts with the push of a button, answers my cell phone, automatically adjusts my seat, maps out my driving route, and has the coveted back-up camera—and I have the security of knowing that if I do get into an accident, trap doors will spring open and not just two, but *multiple*, air bags will rush at me from all sides.

My dogs are still somewhat suspicious of their new transportation. They're not sure about the smaller cargo space which they now have to occupy, and their noses twitch at the new car smell. (I've always wondered if that's real, or some spray the manufacturer uses.)

But together we are breaking it in. And soon their smell will replace the new car spray. As for me, I have already littered the front passenger seat with not one, but two different audio books, reusable shopping bags for the supermarket, and a water bottle. Although, I've been careful about cleaning up after the gum wrappers and pistachio shells, at least so far.

While the inside is beginning to feel homier, the tension still exists around the car's still-perfect exterior and the anticipation of that awful moment when it will acquire its first scratch. And I know it will. Eventually. It's a painful, but inevitable milestone in our relationship.

I think I might be ready to uncover my mirrors and get up from the wooden box, and begin to really enjoy my new car. However, it will take a lot more time before I stop craning my neck!

Other People's Spices

It is July and, once again, we have succumbed to the temptation of a summer rental. Apparently the seduction of a new experience was more powerful than the memory of our last rental.

You see, for our last rental, we had fallen in love with a charming, rustic home on an island with beautiful beaches. At least I *heard* that the beaches were beautiful. For three weeks, I viewed life through a screened-in porch. I was loath to go outdoors for fear of being eaten alive by voracious mosquitoes. Mosquitoes that seemed to thrive on bug spray and had no respect for protective clothing.

But time does have a way of subduing unpleasant experiences. Otherwise, there would be no such thing as siblings, would there? So, here we are again, committed to another three weeks in someone else's house.

Arriving at a rental house is a funny thing. I don't suggest doing it at night. Darkness is not the best time to try to become acquainted with alien light switches. The ones that seem the most intuitive never are. You would think that the switch nearest to the door would turn on the entrance light, but it doesn't. So instead, you trip over your suitcase before you finally find the entrance hall light switch on the adjacent wall.

Although the houses are always clean and ready for our arrival, I invariably feel confronted with the ghosts of former renters. Their presence is usually manifested by what they have left behind: half-used bars of soap and bottles of shampoo or a disposable razor in the shower. But my personal favorites are the treasures that await in the kitchen.

As we entered our current rental, half-empty jars of salad dressing, a bottle of juice, a stick of margarine, and an unopened package of white bread were sitting in the refrigerator. I clicked my tongue and shook my head as I immediately made a judgment about the poor dietary habits of the former tenant. But my immediate dilemma was: What should I do with the food?

I hate to throw food away. But would a partially consumed jar of ranch dressing really make a dent in world hunger? I considered simply pushing it all aside and leaving it as I stowed my own groceries—after all, maybe the next renter would eat margarine. As soon as I closed the door, however, I immediately opened it again, grabbed the old food and tossed it in a garbage bag. I felt cleansed. A little guilty, but cleansed.

A search of the freezer presented the next problem. The freezer was not very large and was already home to several cartons of ice cream, packages of frozen vegetables, assorted breads, and a large bottle of vodka. Hmm. An ice cream and vodka diet. Now *that* was an improvement.

Regaining my momentum, I approached with another garbage bag but then stopped in my tracks. The frozen food might very well have belonged to the owner of the house, I supposed, who might one day return and want the Ben and Jerry's and a Bloody Mary. I refrained from tossing the contents, and rearranged them, instead.

I next took an inventory of the remnants in the pantry and tried to figure out what to do with the vast collection of cooking oils and spice jars contributed by my predecessors. I went on line to research illnesses one might contract from using expired bay leaves and found none. So I decided to keep those and use them as needed.

The kitchen was well equipped, but lacked a few items that I could not live without—and forgot to bring. I told myself they were unimportant, but I knew I would eventually buy replacements, and leave them behind as my contribution to the kitchen's random assortment of utensils, hoping that the person who follows me appreciates a left-handed grapefruit knife.

Our groceries finally put away, and my kitchen survey completed, I feel that I have staked my claim. The space I need is now all mine. I feel satisfied. I have nested in my rental.

It is lunch time and we are hungry. We open what we have brought and begin to prepare sandwiches.

"Where are the knives?" my husband asks.

I look at him amusedly. Did we not enter this house together? I don't recall coming ahead on a scouting expedition. "I really don't know," I answer calmly, "but I bet if we put our heads together, we can find them."

We are now two days into our vacation in our rental home. We have located the knives, but I haven't found anything smaller than a pizza pan in which I can scramble two eggs.

From my personal experience with summer rentals, I find I have a time limit for leaving things as they are. For the short term—say, five days—I can tolerate the mysteries of locating items in a kitchen that is not mine and groping in various drawers for the can opener or the slotted spoon.

By the end of the fifth day, however, I am compelled to begin rearranging things. While I can co-exist with the prior tenants' expired herbs and spices, this open-minded spirit does not necessarily extend to their sense of culinary organization.

It is now day four and my husband comes downstairs for breakfast to find me surrounded by cookware. I've decided to get a jump on things. I have removed every pot, pan, and lid from the cabinets and, with the intensity of Sherlock Holmes, am attempting to match errant pot covers with their mates. Why are there always stray lids? (Whoever can solve this mystery might also be able to explain what happens to the other sock in the dryer.)

After replacing the cookware to my satisfaction, I go to work on the silverware drawer and the illogical placement of knives and cutting boards.

For the moment, I am satisfied. Thus far, I have not found it necessary to rearrange any of the furniture.

I am beginning to think that this time it will work out well. The scenery is beautiful and the insect population somewhat less aggressive than in prior years. We are exploring the countryside and have discovered farm stands where you can buy seasonal produce without little stickers.

I'm looking forward to preparing delicious wholesome meals in the newly organized kitchen and, in anticipation, reread some of my favorite recipes. When I check the inventory of leftover spices, I find that it actually falls short of my needs. Clearly the former tenants have never heard of Jacques Pepin, so I will add some *herbes de provence* and one or two others that eventually will become my ghost in the pantry when the next renters arrive.

Lost in Translation

I know my little saga started on a Wednesday, because that's when *The New York Times* publishes their "Dining" section. It was my husband who saw the editorial about the gadget which promised to make the world's best iced coffee. He knows how much I love iced coffee, which is right up there on my food list next to Cool Whip.

He was very thoughtful, really, tearing the article out of the paper to save it for me before tossing the rest of the pages onto the floor. Throwing the sections onto the floor is his way of communicating to me that they may be discarded. He is a very smart man, though he is, apparently, unable to find his own way to the recycling bin. But I digress.

I read the article, and am surprised to learn that this miracle machine was created in Japan by a Japanese company. I know that I might be stereotyping, but I had never before associated the Japanese people with coffee. Tea, maybe, and definitely saké, but not coffee. Then, again, I probably underestimate the influence of Starbucks on a nation's palate.

In any event, I decide to order the iced coffee maker, and look forward to an enhanced chilled caffeinated experience, rather than the recycled leftover morning brew I usually drink.

Within a week, it arrives. I eagerly tear into the box and remove the contents: a glass carafe, a filter, and a lid. Seems simple enough. Only three components. No moving parts. Nothing to plug in. I spy a small leaflet stuck in the carafe. *Aha, the instructions!* I am psyched, and so are my taste buds.

I extract the leaflet and reach for my reading glasses. A lot of good they will do me, however, since they don't also translate Japanese.

This has to a prank! A poorly-timed April Fool's joke? Is this an oversight, or revenge? Are they still angry over World War II? I do a 360, looking for the hidden camera. *Come on out, son of Allen Funt. I know you're hiding somewhere.*

I turn the paper over, hold it upside down, refold it, then unfold it again. Nope. It's unmistakably Japanese.

I grab for the carton. There are instructions on one of the panels, but they are also in Japanese. Even the illustrations are in Japanese. There are caution warnings with Xs and lines running through the pictures. Not only do I not know what to do, but I have no idea what it is that I'm not supposed to do. The only English words on the box are "Coffee Pot" and "Made In Japan." This already-known-to-me information definitely warrants a *DUH!*

A feeling of helplessness and ultimate frustration has clouded my day. The only thing standing between me and the perfect glass of iced coffee is a series of incomprehensible characters in black ink, which appear to the uneducated as if someone's finger got stuck on the pound key during an overzealous tweet.

I search my brain and can think of no one I know who speaks Japanese. A crash course at Berlitz is instantly dismissed as a viable option. As I ponder what to do next, the proverbial light bulb suddenly goes on. The "aha" moment dawns.

I live in a small, but very savvy, little town that is hip to the benefits of omega-3 fatty acids. We probably have as many sushi bars per capita as Tokyo. (Well, maybe not *Tokyo*, but you get my drift—we have a lot of them per capita.) There has to be a Japanese chef somewhere in this community willing to help me out.

Lunchtime of the following day, I hit my first Asian fusion establishment. I am less than comfortable walking into the restaurant asking only for assistance, so I sit down at the counter and decide it is only right that I order something to eat. To be perfectly honest, although I do enjoy this type of food, I'm not an aficionado and don't know a *futomaki* from a *hosomaki*. When it comes to ordering, I have always depended on the kindness of strangers. Or friends.

I peruse the menu for something that doesn't seem too threatening. As I'm deciding between a California roll and a more ominous-sounding caterpillar roll, the chef approaches. We chat briefly, I place my order, then I shyly withdraw the instruction sheet from my pocket. "I was wondering," I say hesitantly, "can you help me out with these? They're written in Japanese." The poor man's face turns red with embarrassment. He leans forward and whispers to me, "I'm Korean. Please don't tell anyone." I eat my California roll and leave.

Undaunted, I enter the second establishment. I place my order and again question the chef. "Pardon me," I ask, "are you Japanese?" He looks at me as if he is about to say "*duh*." To explain my seemingly stupid question would be to reveal the other man's secret, so I bite my lip. I show him my instructions. He says he's sorry, but he can't help me. While he is of Japanese descent, he was actually born in Brooklyn.

I decide against trying a third time. The spicy tuna *temaki* is starting to repeat on me.

On my way home, it occurs to me that there was a simpler way that would have avoided all this fuss and indigestion: Consult Google! After downing an antacid, I type in the name of the coffee maker and, sure enough, on the manufacturer's website is the English version of the directions for use. I'm excited and happy as I print a hard copy. The elation lasts for the ten seconds it takes me to realize that, while the text is now something I can actually read, all of the essential information regarding measurements is presented in metric units. I'm considering giving up coffee altogether.

Instead, I devote another ninety minutes (I'm no good in math) to refreshing my understanding of solid and liquid measurements, as well as long division. By sheer trial and error, I manage to more or less successfully convert grams and liters into good old patriotic American ounces. Victory is mine!

Was it all worth it? I have to confess that the following day, after the fourteen-hour brewing and refrigeration process, I was treated to the best glass of iced coffee I have ever tasted.

At least that is what I have decided to believe.

I'm still rather incredulous that a foreign-made product could be distributed and sold in the United States without including English-language instructions. But then again, I should be grateful that it was only a simple coffee maker, and not my Toyota!

Domestic Tyranny

I'm sitting here typing and trying to be very quiet. I'm about to write terrible things about my computer and I don't want it to know. I realize I sound more than a touch crazy, but I'm convinced that if I'm not circumspect, and the central processing unit gets wind of what I'm doing, a temper tantrum will ensue, and I will have to endure another major breakdown, like I did last Saturday.

The fact that the malfunction occurred on a weekend, when one is less likely to be able to obtain technical assistance, just goes to demonstrate my computer's capacity for malice. And for so long it had been pretending to be my friend.

We had had a slow build-up of trust over the years. I admit at first I was skeptical, even a little afraid. I have found that, once you reach a certain decade, you don't necessarily welcome innovation into your life—especially innovation that comes with a snake's nest of electrical wires. You find yourself stating emphatically that the way you presently get things done is just fine, thank you very much. And, yes, I suppose I'd have had the same response to the electric typewriter if I'd been the same age when that first appeared.

But gradually, I let myself become convinced that emails were not created by the devil, and there really was a more efficient way to type and save a document.

That's how it began, the insidious process. Little by little, I found myself handing my life over to my computer. I no longer engaged in hand-written correspondence. My beloved set of *Encyclopedia Britannica* was replaced by Google. (I wonder what happened to all those door-to-door encyclopedia salesmen?) Eventually, I made my computer the trustee of my music library and let it serenade me with my favorite songs.

It lured me into allowing it become the keeper of my family photos. Irreplaceable ancestral pictures are now imprinted on its hard drive. Then it gently requested permission to store the contact information of everyone I have ever known in my life, convincing me that my address book was fast becoming a Smithsonian relic.

I started to relax around my computer. I felt we had developed a rapport. I had, by this time, handed over my appointment calendar, my favorite recipes, my buying habits, and my reading preferences.

I was completely primed for the next big step. It wanted my financial information. Who was I to resist the temptation of the eternally accurate bank reconciliation and the draw of on-line bill payment?

Do you see what was happening? How I had been lulled into deeding my life to this machine for the promise of accuracy, convenience, and more space on my bookshelves?

The computer now owns me! It has become my brain. The servant has become the master, like life imitating a British melodrama. It's "*Upstairs, Downstairs* and *Downton Abbey* Meet HAL." (Remember the HAL 9000, the tyrannical computer from *2001: A Space Odyssey*?)

Do I sound slightly hysterical? More than slightly hysterical? Well, that's what it felt like on Saturday morning when I complacently turned on my computer, rightly expecting that it would respond in the helpful manner to which I had become accustomed, only to find myself confronted with nothing. Well, not *nothing* exactly. There was enough something to let me know that my computer, my confidante, my friend wasn't going to operate. That "something" was also known as the "error message."

Error messages alone are enough to cause panic in a Zen master. They are indecipherable by the common man, shrouded in unknown references and secret code numbers. It's the computer acting like it is trying to be helpful, when actually, it's laughing.

My printer, I discovered, was also part of this conspiracy. Overnight, the two had obviously formed a secret pact for the sole purpose of my derailment. The document I had written the day before, which was already late for a deadline, could neither be emailed nor printed. And what about everything else that I had entrusted to this terrorist?

So, there I was, woman on the verge of a nervous breakdown. Me, a highly competent person trained to handle all types of domestic crises. But this was way more than a broken toaster. The only other time I had come close to this degree of casualty was when my coffee maker went on the fritz at six thirty in the morning.

After a series of hysterical phone calls to my son, an IT guy who unfortunately lives in another city, and my Internet provider, it was determined that the hard drive needed to be reconfigured. I quickly recognized that my knowledge of fixing a computer malfunction—which is limited to the unplugging and replugging of a power cord—was insufficient for a catastrophe of this magnitude.

My desktop was holding me hostage, demanding a new name and the option to go wireless. I guess I should be grateful that it wasn't also asking for a helicopter and two million dollars.

I was in desperate need of a hostage negotiator. Although it was the weekend, I took a chance and called my local tech person. Sensing I was suicidal, he was kind enough to give me a Sunday appointment. For his weekend rate, of course. At this point, even the aforementioned two million dollars was not out of the question.

I watched as my computer submitted to his expertise, like an animal to a trainer, knowing it had been bettered. In short order, I heard the welcome sound of my printer forced into submission, as well. Life, as I had come to know it, had been restored, and I was finally able to exhale.

Since the Saturday episode, my computer and I have managed to reestablish a working relationship. I even bought it a brand new router, hoping to soothe the beast within. I have to say that I'm in awe of the degree of dependency I have bestowed on the little monster. And how, each time I push the "Print" key, I expect to be taunted by the voice of HAL, stating: "I'm sorry, Susan, I'm afraid I can't do that."

Spoiler

The sun is shining. The air is comfortably dry—definitely a good hair day. A slight breeze is blowing. Even before I step outside, I can see nature's glory through the windows and I smile. Then I frown. I frown because I suddenly recall the promise I made to myself early this morning just before I rose from my bed. The promise that I would go to the gym today. Instantly, the day grows dark.

It's sad but true. I have become such a gym-o-phobe that even the prospect of donning a sports bra can wreck my entire day. But perhaps "-phobe" is not an accurate suffix to explain my response to this house of dumbbells. I don't exactly *fear* the gym; I out-and-out hate it!

This attitude represents a serious and almost unrecognizable change from my former self. There was a time in my life, extending over many years, that going to the gym was an integral part of my schedule. At least three times a week, there I was, the cardio fitness queen, pounding away on the treadmill and StairMaster. With the fierceness of a warrior, I fought against flab, torturing my individual body parts on machinery that looked like it might have been designed by Torquemada for the Spanish Inquisition.

It was all worth it. I felt virtuous, strong, healthy—to say nothing of gorgeous—as I wore tank tops well into middle-age, flaunting my well-defined shoulders. Michelle Obama had nothing on me. So what happened?

I believe I'm suffering from an acute case of gym burn-out, destined to become chronic unless I can act to reverse it. And you needn't bother to lecture me on the importance of exercise in the "later" stages of life. It won't work. I already read the *Science Times* and revere Dr. Oz.

Although I have succumbed to this workout malaise, I must confess that I have not been able to make peace with my slothfulness. As much as I am repulsed by the sight of a pair of sneakers, I can't seem to silence the little voice that urges me to once again get off my butt. So, heeding the suggestion of well-meaning, more motivated friends, I have, so far, called into play the following strategies:

Scare Tactics. My current behavior is hazardous to my health. Not going to the gym means that I am not striving to ward off osteopenia, or its evil twin, osteoporosis. I will wind up like Sally Field and Blythe Danner, having to take some horrid medication for the rest of my life so my bones don't snap. And the worst of it is, no one will pay me to talk about it on television. I also know that I'm not being kind to my cardio-vascular system, while at the same time depriving my brain of the super-oxygenating results of the elliptical machine. One might think that fear of weight gain would be enough to get me bouncing. And it was—until I learned how long I had to spend working up a sweat to counteract the pleasure of one Oreo cookie. I simply decided to forego the Oreo cookie.

Bribery. A few of my friends who are proponents of retail therapy suggested that I could reward myself if I go to the gym. "It doesn't have to be expensive," one friend said, "maybe a new tee shirt, or a pair of earrings." Now this was an appealing idea that actually got me into my workout attire. Unfortunately, or fortunately, I got completely sidetracked by looking for potential gifts before I actually went to exercise. Eventually it got late enough that I was able to convince myself that I had to go right home because the dogs were starving.

Personal Trainer. Another hopeful suggestion was that I acquire the services of a personal trainer. If I had a specific appointment twice a week, so the theory went, I would not exactly be able to wriggle out of my commitment. This sounded foolproof. So I hired a trainer to come to the house every Tuesday and Thursday at 10:00 AM. She was a lovely young woman, pleasant, dedicated, and very fit. What a wonderful role model. It was good for a while. And, by the third week, I experienced a noticeable shift in my attitude. I no longer hated the gym. I hated the trainer.

Vary the Routine. This was another gem of wisdom from gym-goers; don't keep doing the same old thing. Take classes, so that you always have something new to do. This made sense. I would try to relieve the boredom factor. So I checked the class schedule for the gym I belong to but successfully avoid. "Yogalates"? Don't think I want that one. Sounds like a drink at Starbucks. With soy milk. "Kick Boxing"? Too aggressive. "Zumba"? That sounded goofy enough to be fun. So, with the requisite towel and water bottle I showed up for Zumba. The energetic, slim, instructor with a big voice put on the Latin music and revved up the class. I soon got the feeling that everyone but me had been doing this for their entire lives. They were smoothly going through the routine while I was tripping over my own feet trying to keep up. Oh sure, I worked up a sweat. But it was more from the anxiety of feeling like a klutz than from an active, enjoyable, calorie-burning workout. Luckily, the loud music drowned out the sound of the door closing after me as I quietly slipped away.

Of course, there's always the guilt factor over the money I've spent and wasted on my gym membership. My gym, however, is for the budget-minded, so that's not a powerful guilt. I think that, to get the maximum benefit from the guilt factor, I shall have to join and not attend a much more expensive gym.

And so the struggle rages. The angel on one shoulder telling me to do the right things, while the devil on the left is saying "Hah!" In the meantime, I have stashed all of my tank tops. To borrow a descriptive phrase from Nora Ephron, when a woman reaches that point in life when her cleavage looks like a peach pit, she probably shouldn't be wearing tank tops anyway.

About the Author

Photo by Andrew Kaen

Susan Goldfein holds a doctorate in Communication Disorders from Teachers College, Columbia University, which, while affording her a successful career as a clinician, teacher, and consultant, has done absolutely nothing to prepare her for creating this book.

Nevertheless, she has plunged into a second career writing humorous essays about life with wit, wisdom, and a touch of irony.

Hailing originally from New York City, she currently lives in Florida with her husband and their two senior Yellow Labs, Bette and Davis.

Her essays have appeared in The Palm Beach Post, and have been featured on the Florida Arts Radio Network and the Kravis Center's *Showcase The Writing*. She is the author of the blog "1000 Things to Say Before I Die."